HR How-to

Internal Investigations

Everything you need to know to conduct an internal investigation in the workplace ...

Essential HR Solutions

A WoltersKluwer Company

Publisher: Catherine Wolfe
Editorial Director: Jeanne Statts
Portfolio Managing Editor: Mike Bacidore
Contributing Editors: Jan Gerstein, J.D.
                       Joy Waltemath, J.D.
Production Coordinator: Tina Roselle
Cover Design: Craig Arritola, Laila Gaidulis
Interior Design: Laila Gaidulis
Layout: Publications Design

This publication is designed to provide accurate and authoritative information in regard to the subject matter covered. It is sold with the understanding that the publisher is not engaged in rendering legal, accounting, or other professional service. If legal advice or other expert assistance is required, the services of a competent professional person should be sought.

ISBN 0-8080-0986-9
©2003 **CCH** Incorporated
4025 W. Peterson Ave.
Chicago, IL 60646-6085
1 800 248 3248
hr.cch.com

A WoltersKluwer Company

All Rights Reserved
Printed in the United States of America

Acknowledgements

No book is created by the writers alone. Every book published is a team effort and reflects the dedicated work of each team member.

Our thanks to our team: To Jan Gerstein and Joy Waltemath who served as our team leaders and provided us both insight and encouragement every step of the way. To Elizabeth Pope for her helpful and appreciated editing. To Laila Gaidulis for her unique design and her clever and creative cartoon illustrations. To Craig Arritola for his production assistance and artistic cover design. To Tina Roselle who cleaned up our pages and made sure our words were spelled right and used correctly. To Joyce Gentry who created the index to this book—our own internal investigation.

All we had were words, you all made our words a book.

Cynthia would like to dedicate her work on this book to the memory of her father, Neil.

Cynthia L. Hackerott, J.D.
Lori Rosen, J.D.
June 2003

Contents

Chapter 1	Introduction to conducting an internal investigation	1
Chapter 2	Start with putting together your investigation plan	33
Chapter 3	The investigator	47
Chapter 4	The investigative tools	59
Chapter 5	The interviews	73
Chapter 6	Document, document, document	95
Chapter 7	Reach a conclusion and write your investigative report	109
Chapter 8	Now that the investigation is over	121
	Index	141

Chapter 1

Introduction to conducting an internal investigation

When will you need to conduct an internal investigation?............2
Beginning the investigation.. 11
Initial meeting with the complaining or affected employee........ 13
BEST PRACTICES: Respond to
 misconduct claims like a LEADER 14
BEST PRACTICES: What to
 tell someone who reports misconduct 17
What are the elements of an effective investigation? 18
Investigation guidelines 19
BEST PRACTICES: Consumer
 credit reporting procedures 24
Will interim actions be necessary
 during the investigation? 29
The Quiz.. 30

After a very busy week, you finally have a couple of hours to get to that big stack of "to do" items. Just as you begin to dig in, an employee enters your office and asks if you have a few minutes to discuss a matter concerning a group of coworkers that has made her very upset. You desperately want to tell the employee to come back tomorrow. What should you do?

In addition, you are being sued by an employee who quit two months ago. You've been assigned to investigate the employee's claim of harassment, age and gender bias. The employee's lawsuit states that she was passed over for promotions that were given to younger males and that your superior sexually harassed her by offering job advancement in exchange for social dates. Your job is to find the facts.

1

When will you need to conduct an internal investigation?

Assess the situation

The kind of investigation, if any, that is required will vary with each situation. In some cases, allegations of employee misconduct will not require a full-scale investigation. Sometimes the "investigation" is not really an investigation at all, but an informal discussion that clarifies a misunderstanding. Sometimes, the actual facts are not in question and very little is required in terms of investigating what took place. For instance, an employee may admit to engaging in the misconduct alleged. Even if this is the case, an "investigation" or review should be undertaken before any disciplinary action is taken.

> Federal and state laws require employers to investigate allegations of certain types of alleged employee misconduct, such as allegations of unlawful harassment. This is true regardless of whether the complaining employee has followed the company's formal complaint procedures.

Several situations should prompt an employer to consider conducting an internal investigation. These situations may include:

- an internal complaint;
- a government agency complaint or inquiry;
- a civil lawsuit or criminal complaint;
- an accident or injury investigation; or
- otherwise having knowledge of harassing, threatening, intimidating, or violent and other illegal behavior occurring in the workplace.

Internal complaint

Once an internal complaint is made, an investigation of the alleged conduct should be conducted immediately. This is true even if the complaining employee has not followed the company's formal complaint procedures. The best policy is to investigate all complaints. A company may be advised of a complaint in many ways. Some of the more common ways an issue comes to the company's attention include:

- an anonymous complaint;
- a complaint by another employee or outside party on behalf of a coworker who may or may not be identified;
- a complaint by an affected employee to a member of management which is typically his or her manager or supervisor but who could be, for example, a security guard or nurse; or
- a complaint by an affected employee to human resources.

Anonymous complaint. If the complaint is anonymous, conduct an investigation based on the facts contained in the complaint. Conduct as thorough an investigation as possible and, if the investigation is inconclusive, preserve all records in the event there are subsequent actions.

Complaint by another employee or outside party. If an "interested party" such as a coworker or counselor advises that an employee has been the victim of misconduct or they have observed misconduct, attempt to secure as many facts as possible to enable an investigation. Stress to the individual who is alleging that misconduct is occurring that the company will objectively and confidentially investigate the matter and encourage the affected employee to come forward. If you are told the name of the employee, you must contact the employee as soon as possible.

Complaint made to supervisor or member of management. Frequently the employee's supervisor or leader or another member of management will receive the initial complaint. Taking a complaint to a supervisor may be a difficult and uncomfortable task for an employee and the supervisor. A supervisor should initially react to a complaint by listening, taking the complaint seriously, and being professional and nonjudgmental. The supervisor must then communicate the complaint to HR. Supervisors should *not* decide on their own whether to report the complaint. HR should require that all supervisors funnel all misconduct allegations to the person or people in the organization who are trained and authorized to respond to such complaints.

Complaint made by affected employee to Human Resources.
When an employee asks to meet with you to discuss a situation, you should have an initial fact-finding meeting with that employee right away. The initial meeting with an employee who brings a complaint is a critical stage of the investigatory process. Follow the guidelines for conducting interviews which are covered in Chapter 5.

Government agency complaint or inquiry

A state or federal government agency may investigate your company if it has received a complaint or may conduct an investigation as part of a routine compliance audit. On the federal level, the Equal Employment Opportunity (EEOC) has the authority to investigate complaints of discrimination made on the basis of race, color, sex, national origin and religion, disability and age. The EEOC may also investigate allegations that an employer has retaliated against an employee for objecting to unlawful discrimination.

If you are a federal contractor, an employee may file a discrimination or retaliation complaint against your company with the Department of Labor's Office of Federal Contract Compliance Programs (OFCCP). The OFCCP may investigate such complaints, or may turn them over to the EEOC for investigation. Also, the OFCCP has the authority to conduct compliance audits of federal contractors to assure such contractors are complying with the equal employment opportunity and affirmative action obligations required of federal contractors. These audits are conducted on a random selection basis and can occur whether or not a complaint has been filed against the contractor.

After an administrative agency complaint is filed, you may be asked to provide a statement of position responding to the allegations in the charge. You may also be asked to provide documents or information related to the subject of the investigation. Additionally, the government agency may ask to visit your worksite or to interview some of your employees. When an employer refuses to provide information, or does not do so in a reasonably timely manner, the government agency may issue a subpoena.

The fact that an employee has filed a charge with a governmental administrative agency or the police, does not relieve an employer of the duty to promptly investigate allegations of misconduct and to take necessary corrective action. An agency investigation could take months, or even years, but an employer must investigate and take corrective action promptly. Moreover, an internal investigation will allow you to be appraised of the facts of the situation in order to effectively respond to any administrative agency or police inquiries.

> When an EEOC charge or OFCCP complaint has been filed against your company, you should retain personnel or employment records relating to the issues under investigation as a result of the charge, including those related to the charging party or other persons alleged to be aggrieved and to all other employees holding or seeking positions similar to that held or sought by the affected individual(s). The EEOC Notice of Charge form that you receive should explain the agency's record keeping requirements.
>
> Once a charge is filed, these records must be kept until the final disposition of the charge or any lawsuit based on the charge. (If you are not sure when final disposition has occurred, consult your legal counsel.) When a charge is not resolved after investigation, and the charging party has received a notice of right to sue, "final disposition" means the date of expiration of the 90-day statutory period within which the aggrieved person may bring suit or, where suit is brought by the charging party, the EEOC or the OFCCP, the date on which the litigation is terminated, including any appeals. For more information on documentation, see Chapter 6.

Investigation after receipt of a lawsuit or a criminal complaint

You may become aware of employee misconduct as the result of a lawsuit or criminal complaint filed against your company or one of your employees. Almost anyone can sue your company for some reason. Certainly, employees and former employees can engage the services of an attorney and, generally, sue you for alleged misconduct or harm of some form. The fact that a lawsuit or criminal complaint is filed does not mean you will not prevail; however, it does mean you must investigate and respond. The fact that an employee has filed a lawsuit or complaint with the police does not relieve an employer of the duty to promptly investigate allegations of misconduct and to take necessary corrective action.

HR How-to: INTERNAL INVESTIGATIONS

✓ An internal investigation will allow you to be appraised of the facts of the situation in order to effectively respond to a lawsuit or police inquiry. However, before investigating, discuss the facts with legal counsel. Do not attempt to conduct or participate in internal meetings to "get the record straight" without approval of your attorney. Make sure your attorney understands any concerns or problems you feel exist concerning any aspect of the pending litigation. It is critical that your lawyer knows about any vulnerabilities in your defense.

> **DON'T miss this**
>
> ✓ Avoid retaliation! Immediately upon learning that an individual is suing your firm, take what-ever reasonable steps you can to ensure that the party is not retaliated against in any way. Assuming the individual is employed by your company, there must be no change in the individual's employment situation—no matter how subtle—as a result of the individual's action against the company. Meet with the individual in private, explain the company's desire to ensure that there are no negative reactions, and strongly request that the individual advise you (or the individual he or she meets with) if there is a perception of negative actions. If the individual is no longer an employee, you must still ensure that there are no negative actions directed at the employee by the company. All concerned parties should be advised strongly of the company's firm position against retaliation of any type.

Accident or injury investigations

Accident or injury investigations should be conducted by individuals with specialized knowledge. In large organizations this responsibility is usually assigned to a safety director. In smaller firms, the supervisor of the affected area or employee may be responsible for the investigation. HR is often part of an accident investigation team.

The primary focus of an accident investigation should be on why the accident, injury, or near miss occurred and what actions can be taken to prevent a recurrence. While recommended preventive measures often involve disciplinary actions, discipline is not always the solution. Sometimes the investigation will lead to recommendations for a change in operational procedures or policy.

As part of an accident investigation, the person conducting the inquiry should ask the following questions:

What occurred? The investigation should describe in detail what took place that triggered the investigation. For example, was it an injury to an employee, an incident that caused a production delay, damaged material or any other condition recognized as having a potential for losses or delay?

Why did the incident occur? The investigation should uncover all the facts surrounding the incident. For example, who was involved; was the employee qualified to perform the functions involved; was the employee properly trained; were proper operating procedures established for the task involved. Other issues to look at include whether procedures were followed, and if not, why not; where else does this or a similar situation exist; and how can it be corrected.

What should be done? Identify which aspects of the operation or process require attention. This is not to establish blame, but to determine what constructive actions can prevent further accidents.

What action has been taken? Note any actions already taken to reduce or eliminate accident exposure. Any interim or temporary precautions should also be noted. The investigator should identify any pending corrective action and any reasons for delaying implementation.

Other reasons for conducting an internal investigation

Even if an employee has not filed a complaint or lawsuit, an employer may otherwise have knowledge of harassing, threatening, intimidating, or violent and other illegal behavior occurring in the workplace. Federal and state laws require employers to investigate allegations of certain types of employee misconduct. For example, employers have a duty to take prompt effective action once they have knowledge of a harassment complaint. Although an employer is automatically liable if a supervisor's harassing conduct involves a tangible employment action like a discharge or a demotion, a prompt and appropriate response when employers know of harassing conduct by coworkers will help employers defend against claims of hostile environment harassment.

DON'T miss this

Even if your company policy requires that harassment complaints be made to certain people or be submitted in a specific format (such as in writing), you must act on such complaints regardless of whether the complaint procedures in the company policy are followed.

According to the EEOC, an employer is legally required to investigate an allegation of harassment when ***any*** supervisor has knowledge of the alleged harassment. This obligation exists regardless of whether the supervisor with knowledge supervises any of the employees involved. Employers have a duty not only to the employee making the complaint, but also to other employees who may be adversely affected by the actions of the alleged harasser. Moreover, the employer still has a duty to investigate allegations of misconduct even when the employee has filed a charge with an administrative agency or the police and even when an agency or the police are conducting investigations.

Worst case scenario

Sharon worked as an operator at a chemical plant. She was the only female on her shift. After Sharon was asked to give a talk to a group of girls that would be touring the plant on "Take Your Daughter To Work Day," several of her coworkers stopped talking to her. One coworker told others not to follow Sharon's instructions without confirming with him first. Coworkers also made offensive remarks and played practical jokes on Sharon that made her seem incompetent and jeopardized her safety. One incident involved someone placing in her locker a biblical verse that read, "[a] women should learn in quietness and full submission. I do not permit a woman to teach or have authority over a man, she must be silent." Sharon complained about the harassment to her supervisor, who also witnessed the harassment. She

Chapter 1—Introduction to conducting an internal investigation

also complained during sessions of a company sponsored support group that were attended by her supervisor's boss. Neither the supervisor nor his boss investigated Sharon's allegations and both failed to discipline the co-worker whose behavior toward her was well-known. The only investigation occurred after Sharon found the Bible verse. At this point co-workers were interviewed using a list of yes-or-no questions. The investigation was dropped when the coworkers denied knowledge of the incident. Sharon subsequently brought suit against the company for sexual harassment.

Solution. In a case that went to court with similar facts, the company lost the lawsuit that was filed against it because it failed to make a good faith effort to stop the behavior. In a situation like this, HR must ensure that managers immediately respond to allegations of misconduct to ensure that if a complaint is made, it is investigated. Once HR knows about the alleged misconduct, it must initiate a thorough investigation and take corrective action as necessary. Your company is legally responsible once any supervisor knows about the incident.

Regardless of how HR finds out about it, one of the biggest mistakes HR can make is to ignore or improperly respond to misconduct in the workplace. A worker may be embarrassed or scared about inappropriate behavior and therefore not come right out and clearly say what has occurred. Some employees may not be able to specifically identify any mistreatment they suffer using definite terms, such as harassment or discrimination. In addition, some workers may not wish to label themselves as "victims." Meanwhile HR professionals, concerned about employee privacy rights, are cautious about making additional inquiries. Therefore, it is crucial that HR create an atmosphere where employees feel comfortable raising issues concerning harassing or otherwise discriminatory workplace behavior.

HR How-to: INTERNAL INVESTIGATIONS

> **Example:** Elliott makes repeated negative comments to his coworker, Yelena, about her psychological disability. Yelena may feel uncomfortable talking to HR about the nature of Elliott's comments and instead complain that Elliott "treats her funny" and is "mean" to her. If HR dismisses Yelena's complaint as insignificant and tells her not to worry so much about how others treat her, she probably will not feel comfortable raising the issue again. But if Elliott's behavior is considered unlawful harassment, the employer could be in legal trouble because Yelena complained about the behavior and the employer failed to investigate and take prompt, corrective action.

The delayed complaint

What if an employee reports misconduct that supposedly occurred several years ago? Take the complaint seriously and investigate as you would a current claim. It is possible that the employee cannot go to a government agency or sue in court because too much time has passed under EEOC or other legal rules for filing charges or suing in court. However, HR can never be too sure. Therefore, in addition to the basic information you would ask of the employee making the complaint, also ask if any similar activity has occurred recently. Ask whether some form of retaliation occurred because of the incident. Then investigate to see if other workers have similar complaints.

WHAT you need to know

Experts warn that in many cases there will be a pattern of misconduct by a problem employee or supervisor that is repeated over the years with different employees. Remember that there is no "time limit" on your corporate policy. Regardless of your legal liability, as an HR professional, you know that misconduct can poison a working environment, resulting in increased turnover and lost productivity at the very least. Thus, the passage of time is no reason to dismiss the importance of a complaint.

Beginning the investigation

Be prompt

HR must take prompt action when inappropriate workplace conduct is found. This means immediately doing whatever is necessary to stop the behavior. The potential liability of a company, and in some cases, the personal liability of a manager, depends on the quality, promptness, and fairness of the investigation. Courts have often found that companies have less, and in some cases, no liability if they investigated matters quickly, thoroughly, and fairly. For example, prompt investigation and appropriate remedial action will help prevent employer liability for any sexual harassment that does not result in a tangible job action. Extending the onset of an investigation can traumatize an organization and make witness testimony increasingly unreliable. The quicker the response, the lower the risk of liability. Thus, you must immediately take corrective action that is "reasonably calculated to stop the harassment and deter future harassment."

Even in "victimless" situations—where misconduct was not directly against any specific individual—HR must still take prompt action, or the organization runs the risk of tolerating behavior that is against stated policy. If stated policy isn't promptly and consistently enforced, the organization becomes more vulnerable to charges of discrimination because of inconsistent treatment.

Prompt action by HR sends a clear message to the workforce that inappropriate conduct and other violations of policy will not be tolerated.

Formal or informal investigation?

A formal internal investigation can be time-consuming, costly and take up valuable resources. Therefore, it is HR's job to know the kinds of situations that demand formal investigation and those that can be resolved in a more informal manner. After all, it is to everyone's benefit to reach a solution that is acceptable to all in the most efficient and effective manner.

The kinds of problems that frequently can be resolved informally involve misunderstandings over the organization's policies, standards and work rules. It is the expectations of the organization–often the employee's immediate supervisor–and the employee that are at issue. HR can fairly quickly clarify any misinformation that the employee has received.

On the other hand, an investigation is needed when you don't have all of the facts. A formal investigation is advisable if the situation involves more than one employee, if there is a pattern of unacceptable conduct, if the nature of the conduct is severe, or if you need help from someone with special expertise (Corporate Counsel, Security, Risk Management, Auditors) to reach a conclusion. A formal investigation would also be necessary if you need to examine and review documents and other evidence.

Where to start?

The best place to start any investigation is with the basic facts. The facts of each situation should be carefully analyzed. HR can help direct the focus of the analysis.

- Is Connie's productivity down because she is being careless at her station or because she is pregnant and cannot stand at her post for the time required to complete her quota?
- Are Greg's frequent absences a rule infraction or the result of his medical appointments for the treatment of AIDS?
- Is Jian truly insubordinate or does he just not understand what is being asked of him because of a language barrier?

The answers to these types of questions can help determine whether the situation is disciplinary or whether you're dealing with something else, such as a medical condition that may require accommodation under the Americans with Disabilities Act (and/or a state disabilities law) or a communication problem that could be addressed through better training.

Each rule infraction or allegation of misconduct needs to be carefully looked into. HR can and should help supervisors recommend behavior changes or warn employees when appropriate, but it is equally important that HR makes sure that the reason for the misconduct is not related to a protected trait or right.

If Connie's productivity is down because she is being careless, *if* Greg fails to request leave for his medical appointments, *if* the work rules have been explained to Jian and he comprehends them, *then* these employees should be treated the same way any other employee displaying the same behavior would be treated.

Initial meeting with the complaining or affected employee

Even the first few seconds of the initial meeting are crucial as they set the tone for the entire investigation. Therefore, when an employee comes to you with a complaint, you must be prepared to respond appropriately. To do so, you must understand these three goals of the initial meeting:

Instill confidence. The first interaction with the employee is the time to instill confidence in your ability and that of the company, to address the employee's concerns. Therefore, before questioning the employee, confirm that he or she feels comfortable that you can reach an impartial resolution. Ask, "[I]s there any reason why you feel I cannot be fair and objective?"

Be ready to respond if the employee expresses doubt over your ability to be fair. You may decide to assign the investigation to someone else. Or, at the very least, you can explore the employee's reasons for feeling this way. Starting this dialogue may make the individual feel more comfortable.

Identify all issues. Identify the issues raised by the employee's complaint. This will help you determine whether the issues can be resolved informally or if an internal investigation will be necessary. You must listen carefully, as the real issue will not always be what the person bringing you the complaint says it is. For example, an employee could tell you he has a complaint about his recent performance review . . . and, in response to your questioning, reveal that he and his manager were in a romantic relationship, that he broke it off, and now the manager gave him the bad review as punishment. The issue initially sounded like a performance review problem but is really a sexual harassment problem.

Take the complaint seriously. Take the complaint seriously even if the employee is a chronic complainer or if the behavior doesn't initially seem like misconduct. If the employee quits because he or she has come away with the impression that the company didn't take the complaint seriously, the employer could face a wrongful discharge lawsuit. Refrain from comments like "You're overreacting—I'm sure no harm was intended."

Ask for—but don't require—a written statement. Ask if the complaining employee is willing to provide a signed, written statement of his or her allegation. If that employee is unwilling to provide a written statement, take note of that fact and continue with the interview. Moreover, don't stop investigating the claim. Failure to provide a written statement does not mean that the charge is fabricated; it may just mean that the employee making the complaint is afraid.

Best Practices

Respond to misconduct claims like a LEADER

An effective response to an employee complaint requires the recipient, whether a supervisor or member of the HR team, to act as a "LEADER":

Listen: Create an atmosphere in which employees feel comfortable raising their concerns by taking every report seriously. Listen for code words when someone tells you about someone else's behavior. Does he or she "feel uncomfortable" or "uneasy" in a coworker's presence?

Encourage: Thank the employee for coming forward with a report and try to make the employee feel comfortable by acknowledging the employee's feelings. Reassure the employee that the information will be kept as confidential as possible and that no retaliation will take place.

Ask questions: Get answers. Who did what to whom, when, where, how, and why. Find out what the employee would like to see happen.

Document: Immediately create a written record of the employee's statement. Ask the reporting employee to review and sign your documentation to reflect its accuracy.

Explain: Explain the relevant policy or policies and answer any questions the employee may have.

Respond: Immediately report the conversation as outlined in the relevant policy or policies. If you are charged with the authority to initiate an investigation into the matter, take the necessary steps to do so.

What if the complaining employee requests confidentiality?

What if an employee complains about misconduct but asks that his or her complaint be kept secret? Even if a person who reports workplace misconduct asks that no action be taken, an employer that does nothing in response can be held liable for the misconduct. Moreover, an employer could be held liable if the accused's conduct adversely effects employees other than the complaining employee. Once HR has been made aware of the situation, it must investigate and take any necessary corrective action.

An employee may ask that his or her complaint be kept confidential because he or she:
- wishes to handle the matter on his/her own;
- doesn't want the situation to become public;
- fears being regarded as a "problem employee";
- fears retaliation; and/or
- doesn't want to be responsible for getting the accused in trouble.

However, supervisors and/or HR cannot promise complete confidentiality, and should report all allegations of misconduct to the appropriate person. Supervisors should **not** decide on their own whether to honor an employee request for confidentiality. HR should require that all supervisors funnel all misconduct allegations to the person or people in the organization who are trained and authorized to respond to such complaints.

DON'T miss this

Requiring all supervisors to funnel all reports of misconduct to HR allows HR to review for possible patterns of harassment, discrimination, or other misconduct by the same individual.

Thus, when faced with a request for confidentiality, HR or the supervisor should explain to the employee that the employer has a strict policy forbidding harassment, discrimination and other misconduct in the workplace and has a legal duty to investigate the problem now that it has been raised. Assure the employee that the matter will be handled as discreetly as possible and that no negative employment action will result from the employee's complaint. Then investigate the complaint.

WHAT you need to know

An investigation is obviously hindered if the employee refuses to give any further information about the conduct. This makes it especially important for HR to document the employee's failure to cooperate, document any answers to questions the employee may have provided, and document any further investigatory actions that are taken by the organization. HR should also encourage the employee to come forward again if the harassment continues and follow up with the employee. For more information on documentation, see Chapter 6.

For the reasons explained above, honoring employee requests for confidentiality is extremely risky! However, an employer may choose to honor such a request if the alleged misconduct is not severe, ongoing, or likely to adversely affect others. If you do choose to honor a confidentiality request, be sure to document the complaining employee's request that the complaint be kept confidential and that no action be taken to investigate it. You should ask the complaining employee to sign this document.

Best Practices

What to tell someone who reports misconduct

Lisa Lavelle Burke and Doug Mishkin, attorneys at Patton Boggs, LLP, provided this "to do" list for the initial meeting with an employee who has brought a complaint.

- Thank the person raising the issue for doing so.
- Inform the person raising the issue that the organization does not permit any retaliation or reprisal for bringing a legitimate issue to light, and advise the employee that if he or she believes retaliation is occurring, to report it immediately.
- Tell the employee that if an investigation is needed, he or she will be notified and will be told who will conduct the investigation.
- Tell the employee that you will limit the disclosure to those people having a legitimate reason to know, and instruct the employee to do the same. Inform the employee that he or she, as well as all individuals involved in an investigation, have a duty to keep investigative information confidential.
- Let the employee know that the person conducting the investigation will be getting back to him or her from time to time during the investigation and that his or her continued cooperation in the investigation will be necessary to reach a resolution.
- Ask the employee for suggestions on how the matter could best be resolved. Does the employee have any suggestions? The employee's answer will be helpful to determining how to proceed.
- Let the employee know that while the employer will make a final decision regarding the best way to resolve the issue, the employee's input is valuable and will be considered seriously.
- Thank the employee again for raising the issue and express the organization's commitment to resolving the matter in a timely manner.

What are the elements of an effective investigation?

Effective investigations share certain crucial elements. Attorney Dennis P. Duffy identified the following elements of an effective investigation at the National Employment Law Institute's 25th Annual Conference (2001):

- An immediate response to an employee's complaint (which does not translate into a quick superficial investigation).
- A high quality investigation, which means thorough and complete.
- Permits employees to have a union or other representative present during an interview if an employee asks for representation (see the discussion in Chapter 5).
- An effective computer resource policy to avoid invasion of privacy concerns (see discussion in Chapter 4).
- Awareness that, if using outside investigators, they are subject to the restrictions imposed by the Fair Credit Reporting Act (see discussion on pages 24–25 of this chapter).
- Disciplinary responses that are tailored to remedy the problem at hand (see the discussion in Chapter 8).

Chapter 1—Introduction to conducting an internal investigation

By following these eight general investigation guidelines, employers can increase the overall credibility and effectiveness of their disciplinary system.

1. Establish and use the same investigative procedure for all investigations to ensure "equal treatment under the law."
2. Use an impartial investigator who has knowledge about the employer's policies and procedures.
3. Start an investigation within 48 hours of an incident.
4. Interview the employees involved and all witnesses. Be sure to allow the presence of a union representative or a coworker in an investigatory interview when requested by an employee and required by law.
5. Always document investigative activities, noting the date, time, place and remarks. Employees who are interviewed should be asked to sign the interview summary, sign an acknowledgement or write their own version of the event.
6. Assemble all relevant facts in an objective and fair manner. A time line may help place the facts in context.
7. Gather relevant records, including policies, personnel files and time records. Determine whether further investigation is necessary or desirable.
8. Analyze all data and make a sound decision. Then, write a final report.

Investigation guidelines

General guidelines

Remember the following general guidelines when conducting an investigation.

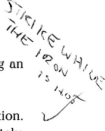

Prompt response. Conduct a thorough and prompt investigation. Begin the investigation as soon as possible, preferably immediately. The quicker the response to a complaint, the lower the risk of liability. Also, unnecessarily delaying or extending the investigation traumatizes an organization and makes witness testimony increasingly unreliable.

Investigator's identity. Determine whether an independent investigator is needed. When a high-level executive is the accused, the independence of the investigation may be questioned in litigation if it is performed by someone who appears to have an interest in vindicating the organization, such as site HR, management, or the organization's own legal department.

Multiple incidents. If there is more than one allegation, treat each incident separately.

Investigate all claims. Although a claim may appear on the surface to be frivolous, treat it as valid until you have established otherwise.

No reprisals. Communicate with interview subjects—inform them of the purpose of the questioning, give assurances that there will be no reprisal for their participation, and obtain participation on a voluntary basis.

Documentation. Develop a complete and accurate written record of the investigation. Take careful notes during all interviews. Try to obtain written, signed statements from the accuser, accused, and witnesses. Retain any other documentation or evidence acquired during the investigation.

Limited access to information. Keep the investigation and the facts that it uncovers under a strict "need to know" basis. Emphasize to all those involved in the investigation—including the complaining employee, the accused and witnesses—the need to keep discussions strictly confidential, backing up these instructions with warnings of discipline if necessary.

Limit the number of persons in the organization who have access to the information. Make sure that all discussions of the matter are in a private area and cannot be overheard. Do not unnecessarily disclose information to witnesses. For example, instead of asking, "Did you see Paul touch Joan?" ask "Have you seen anyone touch Joan at work in a way that appeared to make her uncomfortable?" The purpose of the investigation is to gather facts, not disseminate allegations.

Chapter 1—Introduction to conducting an internal investigation

In discussing the situation with interviewees, make it clear that the facts are not to be discussed with parties who are not directly involved. Warn them of the risk of personal defamation liability if they make malicious or false statements or discuss the matter with others. If there is any doubt about a potential witness' ability to maintain confidentiality, it may be wise to think very carefully before involving that particular witness.

Never broadcast the facts of a given situation or the results as an example to others or as a training tool.

Employers are allowed to question employees about information that relates to an unfair labor practice charge against the employer in order to prepare a defense to the charge. (Unfair labor practices are violations of employees' rights to organize, to bargain collectively with the employer, and to take other action in concert for their mutual aid and protection.) Such questioning cannot be coercive in nature, nor can it exceed the necessities of the legitimate purpose; for example, it can't be used as a "fishing expedition" to find out unrelated information. The employer must follow certain safeguards, including to:

- communicate to the employee the purpose of the questioning,
- assure him or her that no reprisal will take place, and
- obtain the employee's participation on a voluntary basis.

Some experts have suggested similar language be used by an employer when investigating sexual harassment claims. Another expert suggests having interviewees sign a *"Miranda"*-type disclaimer if they may later become adversarial. (A *Miranda*-type disclaimer is a verbal notice to an individual of his or her rights under the law at the time of arrest; you know, "you have the right to remain silent," etc. Here this would ensure that employees know their rights and know that their participation in the investigation is voluntary). Such measures are designed to preserve the integrity of any statements or evidence uncovered during the questioning.

Other important considerations

Good faith should be your guiding principle. Remember that all investigations must be conducted in good faith (in other words, without any preconceived intention to "get" a particular individual). Even if you mistakenly discipline an innocent person, you should be able to avoid legal liability if you conducted the investigation in good faith, arrived at a reasonable conclusion, and implemented appropriate discipline if warranted.

Equal treatment. Fair and consistent treatment of all employees is critical with respect to investigations. Remember that the goal of a proper investigation is *not* to build a case against any particular employee(s). The key question in an investigation should be, "What happened?" rather than "Who is at fault?" Consequently, you will likely have to review and revise your investigation procedures as you go along. Avoid forming conclusions until the investigation is exhausted.

Focusing your investigation on what happened rather than who was at fault is particularly important to keep in mind if other employees in similar situations did not have their actions investigated. Inconsistent treatment could be used as proof that a person was chosen for discharge or other adverse employment actions for unlawful reasons.

When workplace misconduct is not investigated consistently, the organization may not be able to defend itself if faced with a grievance, complaint or litigation. The lack of consistency might be used, for example, to show discriminatory intent, to show that the organization doesn't have employee relations programs, or to show that the organization acted in an arbitrary fashion.

Worst case scenario

Supervisor Sam broke up a fight between a black worker and a white worker and immediately terminated both participants' employment. An investigation by HR revealed that the "fight" was actually an unprovoked attack and that the aggressor was the white employee, who was using illegal drugs at the time. HR also uncovered documentation of a similar, earlier incident involving two white employees. That incident had been resolved by terminating only the aggressor. What should you do? The immediate termination of the non-aggressor employee now appears unwarranted, and, in addition, you have evidence that it could be seen as treating a black employee less favorably than a white employee. Yet the termination already has been implemented.

Solution: Include the organization's legal counsel when a review shows that a termination should not have occurred. You may choose to reinstate the employee who was not the aggressor or negotiate a release. A release is an agreement in which the employee agrees not to take action against the employer in return for some kind of compensation, like money or other consideration of value, such as a neutral reference and other documents. Before reinstating an employee, however, all concerned parties should be consulted. If possible, reassign the returning employee to a different supervisor.

Alternatives. HR can make alternatives available to avoid immediate dismissals and provide additional input or buy some time. In some organizations, a HR professional is available for emergency consultation; other organizations give supervisors the authority to suspend employees and require that they leave the workplace. Another alternative is to permit immediate discharges, but only in limited, specified situations.

After-the-fact investigation. After an immediate dismissal, an after-the-fact investigation should be conducted just as if a termination had just been recommended but not implemented. An exit interview should be scheduled, if possible, and all required notices and paperwork should be completed. During the interview, get the employee's perspective of what happened leading up to and including the actual dismissal. Document carefully and completely. This way, any concerns or problems will be revealed and you will be in a position to eliminate a risk to the organization, even though the action has already occurred.

Fair Credit Reporting Act. The Fair Credit Reporting Act protects individuals' privacy rights in consumer credit investigations and, therefore, has a direct impact on employers who do pre-hire background investigations on applicants. The Act requires employers to (1) disclose that a credit report may be obtained, (2) obtain written authorization from applicants and employees; and (3) provide a copy of the report to the applicant or employee before taking any adverse action based on the report's contents. The law may also apply when an outside organization is hired to investigate sexual harassment or perhaps any other type of disciplinary claims.

Best Practices

Consumer credit reporting procedures

According to an informal staff opinion letter released by the Federal Trade Commission (FTC), employers that hire outside organizations to investigate misconduct claims must follow Fair Credit Reporting Act procedures. Presumably, this analysis would apply to all workplace harassment investigations.

This can present practical problems. First, employers would have to share every aspect of these investigations with the person being investigated, including the sources of all information obtained, before any adverse actions are taken.

Also, employers would be required to obtain prior written consent from any involved employees, provide notice and disclose the scope of the investigation to the employees, and provide a copy of any report. The copy of the report would have to include the sources of all information obtained before any adverse action may be taken.

The FTC offers these recommendations:

Routinely obtain consent at start of employment. An employee's consent to obtaining a consumer report, required by law, can be routinely obtained at the start of employment. This will relieve the employer of the awkward prospect of having to ask a suspected wrongdoer for permission to allow a third party to provide an investigative (or other) consumer report to the employer.

Routinely make disclosures at start of employment. Employers seeking to obtain reports on employees can meet the disclosure requirements in a similar fashion.

Ask all current employees to sign a consent form and provide required notice, all at once. Another way for an employer to comply with these FCRA requirements without alerting a suspected wrongdoer is to ask all current employees to sign a consent form, and provide them any required notice, at the same time.

Conduct investigations internally. The FCRA does not apply to investigations employers conduct themselves through their own personnel. Similarly, the FCRA would not apply where the employer uses a third party that does not "regularly engage" in preparing such reports and thus does not fall under the definition of "consumer reporting agency."

If you must provide a copy of a report prior to adverse action, don't name parties who provided investigative information. To assist an employer who will be asked to provide a copy of a report to an employee prior to adverse action, an investigative agency may draft its report to the employer to minimize risks accompanying disclosure, most importantly by not naming parties that provide negative information regarding the employee.

Take adverse action contemporaneously with providing a copy of the report. The FCRA specifies no fixed "waiting period" that an employer must observe prior to terminating an employee for workplace misconduct based in whole or in part on a consumer report.

Disability-related inquiries. The Americans with Disabilities Act restricts the type of questions that an employer may ask current employees. Employees cannot be asked if they have a disability or about the nature or severity of a disability unless the inquiry is job-related and consistent with business necessity. It stands to reason that an inquiry that is not job-related serves no legitimate employer purpose. However, it does serve to stigmatize the person with a disability.

An employer's belief that an employee's medical condition will impair his or her ability to perform essential job functions, or that the employee's medical condition will pose a direct threat, must be reasonable. This means that it must be based on objective evidence obtained, or reasonably available to the employer, prior to making a disability-related inquiry or requiring a medical examination. Such a belief requires an assessment of the employee and his or her position and cannot be based on general assumptions.

Defining "disability-related". A "disability-related" inquiry is one that is likely to elicit information about a disability. When HR or a supervisor is conducting an investigation in the context of imposing discipline, care must be exercised to not ask questions that will obtain information about a disability. Some of the kinds of questions that are not permitted because they are disability-related include:
- Asking an employee whether he or she has (or ever had) a disability.
- Asking an employee about the nature or severity of the employee's disability.
- Asking an employee to provide medical documentation regarding his or her disability.
- Asking an employee whether he or she currently is taking any prescription drugs or medications, or monitoring an employee's taking of such drugs or medications.
- Asking an employee a *broad* question about his or her impairments that is likely to elicit information about a disability.

The following questions are permitted:
- Asking generally about an employee's well being.
- Asking an employee whether he or she can perform job functions.
- Asking an employee whether he or she has been drinking.
- Asking an employee about his or her *current illegal use of drugs*.

Worst case scenario

John is a manager at a large accounting firm who has been diagnosed with HIV. A partner in the firm, Steven, became suspicious about the nature of John's illness when he found out that a paramedic came to the firm and drew John's blood. To confirm his suspicions, Steven searched John's office and found a letter from Johns Hopkins University AIDS Service and placed it in Steven's personal file.

Solution: Employers cannot do indirectly what they cannot do directly. A surreptitious search of the manager's office is the functional equivalent of a direct inquiry and can result in a lawsuit against the employer for improper medical inquiries under the ADA, as well as for invasion of privacy.

HR needs to help Steven understand why he wants to confirm his suspicions about John's illness. Only if and when Steven legitimately obtains objective evidence that John's condition will impair his ability to perform essential job functions or poses a direct threat to his own health or the health and safety of others would Steven be justified in asking John disability-related questions.

Job-related and consistent with business necessity. A disability-related inquiry may be "job-related and consistent with business necessity" when an employer has a reasonable belief, based on objective evidence, that:

1. An employee's ability to perform essential job functions will be impaired by a medical condition, or
2. An employee will pose a direct threat (to self or others) due to a medical condition.

Known disabilities. Sometimes the standard may be met when an employer knows about a particular employee's medical condition, has observed performance problems, and reasonably can attribute the problems to the medical condition.

> *Example:* For the past two months, Ned has conducted a third fewer audits than the average employee in his unit. He also has made numerous mistakes in assessing whether appropriate documentation was provided in support of claimed expenses. When questioned about his poor performance, Ned tells his supervisor that the medication he takes for his lupus makes him lethargic and unable to concentrate.
>
> Ned's supervisor may ask whether he is taking a new medication and how long the medication's side effects are expected to last. Ned may also be asked to provide documentation from his health care provider explaining the effects of the medication on Ned's ability to perform his job. These inquires may be the beginnings of the organization's efforts at reasonable accommodation.

Third-party information. Disability-related inquiries may also be asked on the basis of reliable information obtained from a third party. Factors that might affect whether or not information that is learned from another person is sufficient to justify asking disability-related questions include:
- The relationship between the person providing the information to the employee about whom it is being provided.
- The seriousness of the medical condition at issue.
- The possible motivation of the person providing the information.
- How the person learned the information (from the person whose medical condition is in question or from someone else?).
- Other evidence that bears on the reliability of the information provided.

Example: Several customers have complained that Magda, a customer service representative for a small mail order company, has made numerous errors on their orders. They consistently have complained that Magda seems to have a problem hearing because she always asks them to repeat the item number(s), color(s), size(s), credit card number(s), etc., and frequently asks them to speak louder. They have also complained that she incorrectly reads back their addresses even when they have enunciated clearly and spelled street names.

Magda's supervisor has a reasonable belief, based on objective evidence, that Magda's ability to correctly process mail orders is impaired by a problem with her hearing. Magda can be asked disability-related questions and/or be required to submit to a medical exam to determine whether she can perform the essential functions of her job.

Will interim actions be necessary during the investigation?

You may need to take interim actions during the investigation to protect the safety of the complaining employee, other witnesses, or the company's property while you conduct the investigation. For example, during the investigation of a workplace harassment complaint, if the alleged harassment is severe (that is, involves physical touching or threats of physical violence), ongoing, or the complaining employee reasonably fears retaliation, the employer could transfer, offer telecommuting, or otherwise separate the complaining employee and the alleged harasser.

However, exercise extreme caution when separating the alleged victim and the accused! If the person making the complaint is reassigned, for instance, to a less desirable position or to a position with few promotion opportunities, the employer may be seen as retaliating against the person for making a complaint.

- ◆ When attempting to remedy harassment, avoid requiring the complaining employee to work less desirable hours or in a less desirable location.
- ◆ If HR offers to transfer the complaining employee, try to get his or her consent and make sure the transfer position is

substantially similar to his or her prior position. This helps ensure that the employee is not being illegally punished for opposing discrimination or harassment.

If necessary, you might be able to transfer the accused or place the accused on **non-disciplinary** leave with pay until the investigation is complete. However, remember to follow proper procedures, such as applicable policies, collective bargaining agreements or civil service rules before taking any action. This will help your organization avoid any due process, breach of contract, wrongful discharge, and/or discrimination lawsuits.

The Quiz

1. When the police or a government agency is conducting an investigation regarding allegations of workplace misconduct, the employer does not need to conduct its own investigation. ❑ True ❑ False

2. An employer does not have to investigate an allegation of misconduct unless the complaining employee follows the organization's complaint procedures. ❑ True ❑ False

3. An effective internal workplace investigation must include:
   a. Prompt response(s);
   b. Fair and consistent treatment of all employees;
   c. Lots of refreshments;
   d. Avoiding retaliation;
   e. Documentation;
   f. All but "c".

Chapter 1—Introduction to conducting an internal investigation

4. Individual supervisors should **not** be allowed to independently determine whether to honor an employee's request to keep a complaint confidential.   ❑ True   ❑ False

5. Employees cannot be asked about if they have a disability unless, the question is:
   a. Asked politely;
   b. Asked by a supervisor;
   c. Job-related and consistent with business necessity; or
   d. Phrased according to company procedures.

Answer key: 1. F; 2. F; 3. f; 4. T; 5. c.

Chapter 2

Start with putting together your investigation plan

Start early 34
Understand the purpose of the investigation 34
Places everyone! Script your investigation plan 35
BEST PRACTICES: How to prepare your investigation plan 36
Gather only the facts about what happened 39
What are the potential consequences of the investigation? 43
Interview all relevant persons 44
The Quiz 45

> *Abra is at her wit's end. The teasing she endures each day at work has gotten so bad she is missing work to avoid it. She has also left work in tears at least once a week for months now. She tried talking to the coworkers who are taunting her. She tried talking to her manager. She even consulted with a therapist via your EAP, but the end result is the same—she is miserable and unable to do her work.*
>
> *As a last resort, Abra has filed a grievance, claiming she cannot work in this hostile work environment. The complaint ended up on your desk for investigation.*
>
> *Where do you begin your investigation?*

Start early

To be relevant, an internal investigation must begin as soon as you are made aware of the need. Don't delay. Your facts and the recollections of people you will need to talk to during the investigation will not get any fresher than they are right after you determine an internal investigation is needed.

Keep in mind that an early resolution to the investigation benefits the organization and the person bringing the complaint—to the extent that the investigation requires people to be away from their regular work and disrupts business, you want a swift conclusion. Acting promptly shows the person bringing the complaint that you are taking it seriously and working on a conclusion.

An immediate response to a complaint does not, however, translate to a quick, superficial investigation. Take the time needed to make the investigation thorough and complete.

> Try to begin within 48 hours of receiving a complaint whenever possible. Set a reasonable but direct time line and don't drag your feet. Understand that a swift conclusion to the investigation is in everyone's best interest.

Understand the purpose of the investigation

As you saw in Chapter 1, there are many reasons an organization would need to conduct an internal investigation.

Understanding the nature of the complaint sets the plan and requirements of the investigation. If you receive a complaint from the EEOC or OFCCP, you will know where to begin in planning your investigation. If the complaint comes directly from the employee, take time to understand the nature of the complaint so that your investigation encompasses the entire issue and not only a small part of it.

Let's go back to the opening scenario for a moment. Abra complained that her coworkers were teasing her so badly that she dreaded coming to work and was having tension headaches. Things are so uncomfortable for her she filed a complaint in your HR department. As you begin your investigation of her complaint, make sure you understand the nature of the harassment that she alleges:

Chapter 2—Start with putting together your investigation plan

- Is it sexual harassment?
- Is it incivility?
- Is it based on her gender, religion or skin color or other discriminatory behavior?
- Is it based on her country of origin or her inability to speak English well?

Or is it a combination of these or other factors? Take time in your first discussion with Abra to know what she feels is going on before jumping to any conclusions, including what you are investigating.

Places everyone! Script your investigation plan

Prepare for your investigation in advance. Don't just jump into it. Have a plan of action. You don't need to reinvent the wheel each time an investigation is required. Have a standard investigational plan or script and adjust it as needed for each individual case.

✓ Checklist
Scripting your investigation
Consider the following points in preparing your plan:
- ☐ What is the purpose of this investigation?
- ☐ Who will conduct the investigation? Who will that person report back to?
- ☐ Who will you need to talk to?
- ☐ What are the potential consequences for the conduct being investigated?
- ☐ What evidence needs to be collected?
- ☐ What policies or work rules are involved? Do you have copies of those policies or rules?
- ☐ What records or reports will you need to see?
- ☐ What investigational tools will you use? Searches? Drug or polygraph tests?
- ☐ What is your time frame for completing initial interviews? Follow-up interviews?
- ☐ Who will create the final report summarizing the investigation and the recommended action?

Have a script for your investigation, but write it in "pencil" to maintain the needed degree of flexibility. Know that adjustments will need to be made to the plan as the investigation proceeds, so always expect the unexpected!

Best Practices

How to prepare your investigation plan

Begin your investigation by role playing, suggests Stephen Paskoff, Esq., president of Employment Learning Innovations, Inc. of Atlanta, Georgia. In his session at the Society for Human Resource Management conference, Legal Sleuthing: Investigative Tools for Finding Facts Fairly, Paskoff told attendees to imagine that they were the jurors selected to hear the employee's case. "Think like a juror," Paskoff recommends. "That's who will decide the case."

- What does a juror want to know?
- What are the issues in the case and what information do I need to analyze the issues?
- What information will you as the manager want to gather that will satisfy you as the juror?

Paskoff provides a model to use entitled "Let's Please Discover What Occurred." There are five segments to the model:

- **Law/policy:** What does the law or company policy say about the event in question? Include applicable policies as part of your investigative file.
- **Parties:** What do the involved parties say occurred? Interviewing both sides is vital to establishing a fair investigation.
- **Documents:** What do the documents indicate? Collect all documents relevant to the claim. Include performance appraisals, exit interview forms and any other company documents that may help uncover the facts surrounding the employee's claim.

Chapter 2—Start with putting together your investigation plan

- **Witnesses:** Are there witnesses to the event or behavior in question? As you conduct your investigation, keep detailed records of testimony from eyewitnesses.
- **Other cases:** How were similar situations handled by your company in the past? Consult HR and legal departments for documentation or company decisions surrounding these events and keep a copy in your file. As you carefully consider the similarities, always ensure that your decisions are fair and equitable, not merely convenient.

Remember your role as a juror. If you have not made a fair investigation, you will not succeed in convincing the jury or the juror that the evidence is fair. While the goal is to have an outcome that is favorable to the company, your job is to make a fair and complete investigation of what occurred.

If you bypass unfavorable evidence, testimony or documentation, be certain that the opposition will not.

DON'T miss this

Worst case scenario
Be consistent—"Do it for one, do it for all"

Mali, an excellent draftsperson, comes to Susan, an HR professional. He complains to her about the man at the next drafting table, Tim. Tim, Mali tells Susan, is a racist and makes degrading remarks about the ethnic group that Mali's family belongs to. Mali is infuriated with Tim's remarks and callousness. He wants Susan to do something about Tim.

Susan knows what a great employee Mali is and that he would not complain about Tim's behavior unless it was offensive to him. She sympathizes with Mali over his discomfort and arranges to have Tim moved to another section where drafting is done.

38 HR How-to: INTERNAL INVESTIGATIONS

Weeks later, Rhianne comes to Susan. Tim is now in her section and is harassing her in pretty much the same way he harassed Mali. Rhianne is new and nowhere near the draftsperson that Mali is. Susan dismisses her complaint with a quick, "That's the way Tim is. You'd better get used to it."

Solution: Two strikes against Susan in the above example. Instead of acting in Mali's favor or dismissing Rhianne's concern, she should have listened to each person's story and investigated the complained of behavior.

In each case she jumped to a conclusion with no investigation, but even worse, under the same types of circumstances, she took radically different action. Followed to its logical—and too often actual—conclusion, Rhianne will sue for discrimination based on that differential treatment.

Be sure to treat every complaint the same. Give it a careful investigation and an equal investigation. Keep records of what steps were taken for different categories of investigations (harassment, discrimination, theft, misuse of company property, etc.) and follow the same steps the next time that type of behavior is investigated. The consequence for uneven handling of complaints is a day in court ... something every organization and every manager wants to avoid.

Avoid harassment, discrimination and unfairness in your investigations.

Gather only the facts about what happened

Assemble all of the relevant facts surrounding the complaint in an objective and fair manner. Use a timeline to place the facts in context. Make sure that you are not using the facts to support a predetermined conclusion. The purpose of the investigation is to uncover the facts, not to prove your theory of what happened.

Have a clear scope for your investigation and stay within it. Don't wander off on tangents and cloud the relevant facts with irrelevant ones. If need be, keep a written reminder of what the scope of the investigation is with you at all interviews and refer to it as the interview moves along. If you have set reasonable boundaries for your investigation, it will be a much better effort.

Evaluate the facts that are presented to you. Discard those that are not relevant. List those that are relevant on your timeline and make sure you know their source. Ask yourself the following questions as you proceed:

- Are any facts vague? Check them out further.
- Are any facts contradictory? Go back and see if you can resolve the contradiction. If not, clearly label the facts as contradictory.
- Are any facts really rumors? Substantiate them or reconsider their use.
- Are there facts you wish you had? Search for them further!

Be clear in your mind what is a fact, what is an opinion, what is a guess, what is a conclusion and what is hearsay (something a person knows only by virtue of having heard someone else say it without independent verification).

> **Example.** *In an interview Harmon tells you that Tankia has been stealing equipment from the computer room. "How do you know?" you ask Harmon. "Jessup told me," is his reply.*
>
> *Harmon's statement is hearsay. To make it a "fact" you would need to interview Jessup and elicit his eyewitness account of what he saw regarding any theft of computer equipment by Tanika.*

What is a fact? A thing presented as having objective reality. There's that word again: OBJECTIVE.

The facts must speak for themselves and not be conclusions based on circumstances. If they are conclusions based on circumstances, go back and investigate further to see if you can get to their objective reality. And even when the facts are objective and fair, ask yourself if they are relevant to this investigation!

Chapter 2—Start with putting together your investigation plan 41

Worst case scenario
Gather all of the relevant records

Remember Abra from the introductory scenario? It ends up her complaint is one of sexual harassment. She alleges that her coworker, Don Juan, keeps asking her for dates and making suggestive comments about her attire and shape. She told you that she turned down his invitations to have a drink or go to a movie and his lewd suggestions for copy room activities they could share. She also told you that she had e-mail messages in which "DJ" described his vision of their nights together and notes he left on her desk asking for dates.

Abra also told you that three women, upon seeing "DJ" hanging around her desk, told her he'd been pestering them to go out with him as well.

When you interviewed "DJ", he was shocked that Abra misinterpreted his joking around and he sincerely promised you it wouldn't happen again. He sheepishly told you he liked Abra and did ask her out once but that she'd turned him down and he'd stopped trying.

Concluding he was sincere, you let him know that if he bothered Abra again he'd be in real hot water, and you dismissed the complaint as a misunderstanding. You relayed this information to Abra, told her it was just a misunderstanding and that the matter was closed. Weeks later Abra quit and sued the organization and you personally based on sexual harassment.

Solution: Where did you go wrong? In this case, among other things, you did not collect the relevant records that came up during the interview with Abra. If you'd gathered the e-mail messages and notes, you would have seen that there was more than one occasion that "DJ" pressed his intentions on Abra and you would have seen the inappropriate nature of the messages and notes. Seeing those records, your investigation would very likely have come to a different conclusion.

You also did not gather all of the facts and interview all of the relevant witnesses—for example, the three other women Abra told you about– before concluding your investigation.

What kinds of records should you be interested in as you plan and implement your internal investigation?

✓ Checklist

Records relevant to an internal investigation
- ☐ Agendas/itineraries
- ☐ Communications to employees
- ☐ Complaints
- ☐ Computer files—even deleted ones
- ☐ Expense reports
- ☐ Instructions
- ☐ Logs
- ☐ Managers' notes & files
- ☐ Memos or notes about specific incidents
- ☐ Performance appraisals
- ☐ Personnel files
- ☐ Policies
- ☐ Procedures
- ☐ Receipts
- ☐ Samples of work
- ☐ Security records
- ☐ Time records
- ☐ Training records
- ☐ Travel documents
- ☐ Written rules

Treat your records as any other piece of evidence you gather for your investigation. Keep them organized and identified as to date and source. Keep them confidential and only share them with those who have a need to know—that will usually not include parties to the investigation. Make sure you keep them in a secure location and do not leave copies lying around or allow them to circulate.

- ◆ Records = evidence
- ◆ Evidence = Facts
- ◆ Facts = Path through your investigation.

Chapter 2—Start with putting together your investigation plan

What are the potential consequences of the investigation?

What can happen as the result of an internal investigation? There are several possible outcomes:
- No adverse employment action is taken because no discrimination or harassment or inappropriate behavior is found.
- A warning is issued along with a clear message about the expected behavior in the future.
- Some adverse employment action short of termination is taken—suspension, demotion, formal reprimand.
- The accused employee is terminated.

Based either on your organization's policy or law, what type of action is required if the investigation shows that the complained-of behavior did happen? Check state and federal law for any penalties or remedies they may contain or consult with legal counsel.

Carefully review your organization's policies and practices. What has been done under these same circumstances in the past? Make sure any potential consequences are clearly understood by both the person registering the complaint and the accused.

> **Example.** Sarrae filed a complaint with HR alleging that although she had more seniority and more training, Dirk was promoted to assistant project manager and she was not. According to her complaint, she was passed over because she's a woman. She also gave several other instances when her manager promoted men when women should have been promoted.
>
> An investigation concluded that Sarrae was unfairly passed over for the promotion. A decision was made to (a) give the next assistant project manager job to Sarrae and (b) to take her manager out of a management position.
>
> When you met with Sarrae to tell her the result of the investigation, she was horrified to learn that her manager had been demoted. "I didn't want to have that happen!" she exclaimed, "I just wanted the promotion I deserved. You can't demote Luis on my account. I want to withdraw my complaint!"
>
> Had the potential consequences of the complaint been explained to Sarrae at the outset, the decision to demote Luis

How-to: INTERNAL INVESTIGATIONS

> would not have come as a surprise to her. She would have understood that if discrimination was found, company policy would require that Luis be taken out of a management position for going against the company's fairness policy.
>
> The idea here is not to base filing or not filing a complaint on the potential consequences of the investigation, but to fully inform the parties as to the potential outcome.

Make the potential consequences—all that might apply—a part of your investigation plan. Talk about the potential consequences with each person you interview. Make them part of the record you create for your investigation.

The purpose of the investigation is to uncover the facts about what happened with regard to a complaint. The investigation is not designed to justify your conclusion or the consequences that your conclusion leads to. The investigation is to see whether complained-of behavior happened and if it did, to remedy the wrong that was done.

Spell out the potential consequences for the conduct being investigated.

Interview all relevant persons

Start by interviewing the employee who has complained, the accused employee, and other witnesses who may have relevant information. Be sure to ask each person you interview if there are others that they are aware of who have information that could help in this investigation. Don't just assume the person bringing the complaint or the accused has given you all of the names you will need to make your investigation meaningful. When you do follow-up interviews, especially with the complaining employee and accused employee, ask again if there is anyone else you should be talking to—perhaps another name or conversation will have come to mind.

Chapter 2—Start with putting together your investigation plan

> Review the people to be interviewed:
> - Who will be combative?
> - Who will be cooperative?
> - Who will be sympathetic?
>
> Adjust the interviewing technique according to the individual's emotional disposition.

Immediately arrange to interview witnesses. Employees who are amenable to cooperating in an investigation may, for any number of reasons, present difficulties at a later time. What happened may grow fuzzier as time goes on and facts may become unclear. You can always reinterview a witness at a later date, but you will get the freshest information early on in the investigation.

Ask for leads! *Ask each person you interview whether he or she is aware of any other witnesses. Ask each person you interview if there is any other relevant information or evidence that you may be missing.*

The Quiz

1. An internal investigation should be started within 48 hours of receiving a complaint. ❏ True ❏ False

2. All internal investigation should be conducted in an identical fashion, no matter what their underlying purpose. ❏ True ❏ False

3. Consistency is not an element of internal investigations because each investigation is separate and unique. ❏ True ❏ False

Continued on next page

Continued from previous page

4. The only relevant people you need to interview as witnesses are the employee who has complained and the accused employee. ❏ True ❏ False

5. Determine the consequences of the investigation only after the facts have been gathered, the interviews have been completed and a conclusion is reached. ❏ True ❏ False

Answer key: 1. T; 2. F; 3. F; 4. F; 5. F

Chapter 3

The investigator

First & foremost, choose someone impartial 48
Legal requirements for investigators 49
Can this person communicate well? 50
Using staff members as investigators 51
Bringing in outside investigators 52
Using a legal advisor 55
How many investigators will you use? 57
BEST PRACTICES: Choose the number of investigators 57
The Quiz 58

> *Hava filed a complaint alleging gender bias, discrimination based on national origin and religious discrimination. Hava comes from the Middle East and speaks with an accent.*
>
> *HR selected Keenan to investigate Hava's complaint. Keenan resents anyone who doesn't speak English well and was once reprimanded for treating women badly in the workplace. In addition, Keenan had a bad experience in the Gulf War and thinks all Middle Easterners are less than truthful.*
>
> *After two days, Keenan handed in his conclusion that Hava's allegations were unfounded. When a meeting to discuss the conclusion of the investigation was held, Keenan's prejudices were revealed and a new investigation was required. What steps should HR have taken to ensure an impartial investigation?*

First & foremost, choose someone impartial

What qualities should someone have who is selected to conduct an internal investigation? First and foremost, select someone who is impartial. An impartial person has no stake in the outcome of the investigation—including a preference for one side over the other—other than finding out what occurred. The investigator you select can be an employee of the organization or someone from the outside. No one is without opinions, but the investigator needs to be someone who can separate his or her own feelings and preferences from the task at hand.

WHAT you need to know

The investigator must come to the investigation without a preconceived notion of what the outcome "should" be. It is the investigator's job to collect evidence, talk to witnesses, review policies, procedures and rules, look at the records and come to a conclusion based on those factors. It is not the investigator's job to decide at the outset of the investigation who's right and who's wrong and then find ways to support that decision with evidence.

Clearly, the investigator cannot be someone who is in some way associated with the complaint. If Hava is complaining that she was discriminated against by her manager, and the head of HR is one of the witnesses Hava points out as having knowledge of that discrimination, that HR director cannot be selected to be the investigator for Hava's complaint.

✓ Checklist

Who should not be selected to head up an internal investigation?

Even if they are not involved in the circumstances surrounding the complaint, the following individuals should not be selected to be the investigator as they might not be impartial:

- ☐ The complainant's or accused's
  - ☐ Direct supervisor
  - ☐ Coworker
  - ☐ Relative
  - ☐ Close friend or known "enemy"
- ☐ Someone with a known prejudice for one outcome or another
- ☐ Someone with a known prejudice for or against one group of people.

An objective third party should be selected to be the investigator. Investigators must be impartial, must be perceived as impartial and must have knowledge of the employer's policies and procedures.

DON'T miss this

Legal requirements for investigators

Qualification for EEOC Investigation. Equal Employment Opportunity Commission (EEOC) investigators for federal agencies must have 32 hours of initial training on EEOC laws, the federal EEOC process, remedies, case management issues and investigative techniques. In addition, eight hours of continuing training is required annually.

EEOC investigators for some state agencies must meet minimum training or experience requirements.

> Even if there are no legally mandated training requirements for investigators, if your investigator is not trained or not trained sufficiently, he or she is an easy target for legal action if the complainant does not like the outcome of the investigation and sues.

Some states require that investigators who are not employees of an organization be licensed by the state.

California, Texas and Maryland require that third-party investigators (outside investigators) possess a private investigator's license if they are investigating employee misconduct. No license is required if the investigator is an employee or in-house counsel.

Virginia requires that third-party investigators of "civil wrongs" have a private investigator's license. "Civil wrongs" may include allegations of employee misconduct. Again, employees and in-house counsel are exempt from the licensing requirements.

Can this person communicate well?

Being impartial will not in and of itself ensure a good investigation. The investigator must also be a good communicator. In the course of the investigation, the investigator will need to talk to many different people. Understanding how to talk to people with different temperaments will be essential.

- Some will be shy and need to be drawn out
- Some may be hostile, angry or otherwise uncooperative
- Some will have good memories, others will not remember events and facts
- There will be those who are people pleasers and want to tell you what they think you want to hear
- Language may be a barrier and you may need to speak through an interpreter
- For some talking to the investigator will be easy, for others difficult
- There will be different levels of education and skills

Chapter 3—The investigator

The list is as endless as there are people to be interviewed. Each will be different and will require a different set of skills to interview. To get the best results, the interviewer needs to be someone who is good at drawing out different personality types.

In addition, the investigator will need to be able to communicate his or her conclusion, both orally and in writing. So the investigator must be proficient in those skills as well.

Using staff members as investigators

Most commonly if you use an inside investigator—staff member—he or she will be part of your Human Resources (HR) team or an Equal Employment Opportunity (EEO) officer. Being part of your organization, these individuals understand your organization's culture, employees and workplace dynamics better than an outsider would. On the other hand, for the same reasons, an inside investigator is more easily a target for accusations of bias than is an outsider.

> *Who should investigate?*
>
> *In many cases, HR or another staff member of your organization will be responsible for the investigation. Be sure the person you select is thoroughly trained before being assigned investigative duties.*
>
> *Training should include learning the skills that are required for interviewing witnesses and evaluating credibility.*

DON'T miss this

The greatest advantage to using a staff member to conduct your investigations is that person's familiarity with your organization's policies, practices, procedures, personnel and past. If a similar complaint was lodged before, your staff member may well be aware of it and what action was taken. This is important in preserving the fairness aspect of the investigation—that similar circumstances be treated similarly.

✓ Checklist

Characteristics of a good investigator

Knowing something about the investigator's mindset is helpful. Is the person known to be:

- ☐ Discreet
- ☐ Unbiased
- ☐ Evenhanded
- ☐ A good communicator
- ☐ Good at keeping to a tight schedule
- ☐ Respected by others
- ☐ A clear thinker

Remember Keenan from the opening scenario? Being part of the organization that selected him, he never should have been selected in the first place as his previous reprimand for mistreating women should have been part of his work history.

Bringing in outside investigators

While knowing the culture he or she is investigating may help an investigator, there are advantages to selecting someone who will come into the workplace only to conduct the investigation and will then leave. Using an outside investigator will help avoid the awkward feeling on the part of the accused or the complainant every time they see the staff investigator in the workplace. Worrying about having to see the investigator and knowing what that person knows about them may even keep people from either bringing legitimate complaints or acting as witnesses.

Chapter 3—The investigator 53

Worst case scenario

Rhia and her coworker Trish were at a bar with a number of people from work one night. Both women were drinking heavily and Rhia was "coming on" to Benjie, a male clerk she supervises. Trish was aware that Rhia had been making advances to Benjie for months, asking him out, leaving love notes on his desk and trying to get him to go out with her. Trish had even heard Rhia tell Benjie that if he turned her down again he'd be sorry!

Carl, an HR staff member, has been selected to head the internal investigation into the sexual harassment complaint Benjie brought against Rhia. Benjie had identified Trish as a witness who heard Rhia threaten him if he didn't date her.

Trish wants to do the right thing, but is afraid that if she tells Carl what she knows and it gets out later there may be repercussions on her marriage. Her husband also works at the same facility and doesn't know Trish has been bar hopping with Rhia. It's not that she has reason to doubt Carl's ability to keep information private, but she's seen it happen too many times that information that was supposed to be confidential gets out.

Solution: Having an outside investigator could well have made Trish a more willing and forthcoming witness.

✓ Checklist
Advantages to bringing in an outside investigator

- ☐ Knowing that he or she will not have to "live" with either the accused or the accuser after the investigation may help the investigator remain impartial.
- ☐ The outside investigator has no previous experience with any of the parties involved and so comes to the investigation without the kind of prejudices that arise from knowing someone's past performance or history.
- ☐ Witnesses may be more forthcoming with an outsider, not having to fear that what they tell the person may someday become "conversation around the water cooler."
- ☐ Using someone from an outside investigation firm may benefit your investigation as they could be familiar with the type of investigation you are making and have questions to ask or tools to use that you might not have thought of internally.
- ☐ The outside investigator will be brought in specifically for the purpose of carrying out the investigation and will not require that someone from your organization find time within his or her schedule to do the work.

Fair Credit Reporting Act governs outside investigators

According to two advisory opinion letters issued by the Federal Trade Commission (FTC), the Fair Credit Reporting Act (FCRA) notice and delay requirements apply to outsiders who investigate workplace misconduct.

If an organization uses an outside investigator who **regularly** conducts investigations, the organization must:

♦ Notify the target of the investigation in writing that it would like to use an outside investigator to investigate allegations involving the employee.

> - Inform the target of the investigation of his or her rights under the FCRA.
> - Obtain written consent to use an outside investigator from the target of the investigation before starting the investigation.
> - Before taking adverse employment action, give the target of the investigation a copy of all investigative materials in the file.
> - Before taking adverse employment action, give the target of the investigation the opportunity to dispute any perceived inaccuracies in the report.
>
> The FCRA applies to any investigator who is not employed by the organization.

Using a legal advisor

In some organizations, HR may coordinate investigations with an in-house attorney. Also, HR may coordinate with the security department, especially if those departments contain staff with prior law enforcement background and training.

*Do not choose your in-house counsel as your investigator **just** because he or she is a lawyer! Make sure your investigator knows the law relevant to the investigation being undertaken. More critically, make sure he or she knows how to conduct an investigation.*

DON'T miss this

Another alternative is to ask an outside attorney to conduct the investigation. Although an expensive option, putting an attorney in charge of a workplace harassment investigation may show that the organization wants objectivity and is concerned about the seriousness of the charge. In the event the charge is against a senior member of management, utilizing outside attorneys may be the best strategy to avoid conflict of interest charges.

WHAT you need to know

Consider pairing an HR staff member with legal counsel for a thorough and complete investigation. Having an attorney assist in the investigation presents several advantages:

- If the complaining party later sues your organization, documents created during the investigation are generally protected from disclosure to the complaining party in any future lawsuit in which the lawyer-investigator is not also the defense attorney.
- An attorney knows the "ins and outs" of the law and can help ensure that legal issues that are raised during the investigation are explored thoroughly, protecting the organization from later claims of violation or abuse of the law.
- The attorney is not involved with employees—directly or indirectly—and can serve as a neutral third party in the investigative process.
- The attorney is likely to be seen as impartial by all parties as he or she represents the company and not one side or the other to the complaint.

Remember that if you use your corporate counsel as your investigator, he or she will likely not be able to represent your organization at trial if the matter ends up in court. Why? Because the same person generally may not be both an advocate and a witness at trial. In almost every instance, the investigator will be called as a witness if the investigation ends up in court and will not, therefore, be able to serve as your counsel in court.

Finally, when considering using your corporate counsel as an investigator keep in mind that doing so destroys the usual guarantee that communications between an attorney and his or her client remain confidential—this is often referred to as the "attorney-client privilege". The attorney-client privilege usually allows an organization to prevent the disclosure of documents and communications between the organization and its attorney about certain things, for example, legal strategy. These documents and communications generally will be "discoverable"—that is, the employee's lawyer will be able to require you to produce those documents and communications during the litigation process—if your lawyer created the documents and made the communication while acting as your investigator.

How many investigators will you use?

Throughout this chapter we have been referring to "an investigator." There are varying schools of thought about having one investigator or more than one. The majority of time, one investigator is used, but there are times when more than one—but not more than two—may work better. Consider the following advice:

> ### Best Practices
> **Choose the number of investigators**
> Michael Johnson, J.D. and Andrew Foose, J.D. provided these guidelines for deciding how many investigators to use in your internal investigation:
>
> **One investigator**
> - Cheaper
> - Consistency of questioning
>
> **Two investigators**
> - Can corroborate what happened in the interviews if a witness later disputes what was said
> - Can compare impressions of the case and bounce ideas off each other
>
> **More than two investigators**
> - Don't use. Often makes it much harder for the witness to feel comfortable during the interview
> - You want to feel like witnesses are having a conversation with the investigator, not testifying in front of an audience
>
> *Source: 2003 Brightline Compliance, LLC*

If you use two investigators, one person should do the questioning while the other takes notes. Jumping back and forth between two investigators can distract the flow of questioning.

The Quiz

1. The investigator should be someone who knows the complainant and accused well, for example, someone who works with them. ❑ True ❑ False

2. A good investigator has which of the following characteristics:
   a. Is discreet
   b. Is impartial
   c. Is knowledgeable about the subject being investigated
   d. Is a good communicator
   e. All of the above

3. While the investigator needs to be a good oral communicator, he or she does not have to have good writing skills. ❑ True ❑ False

4. It is good strategy to use your in-house counsel as your investigator as it will prevent the other side from seeing documents created during the investigation if the matter goes to trial and that attorney is not also representing the organization at trial. ❑ True ❑ False

5. The investigator could be:
   a. An employee of the organization
   b. The organization's attorney
   c. An outside person
   d. Any of these

Answer key: 1. F; 2. e; 3. F; 4. F; 5. d

Chapter 4

The investigative tools

The investigation toolbox 60
"An expectation of privacy" 60
BEST PRACTICES: Curbing that expectation of privacy 61
Interviews 62
Searches 62
Polygraph testing 67
Drug testing 69
The Quiz 72

> *Amman is investigating a complaint of misconduct brought against Jo-Lee. Jo-Lee allegedly took office supplies from the company's stock over a three-year period.*
>
> *As part of his investigation, Amman intends to search Jo-Lee's locker, e-mail and backpack. While Jo-Lee acknowledges the company's right to search her locker, she disputes that it can search her purse or e-mail files. Those, she claims, are her private property.*

The investigation toolbox

As you plan out your investigation, decide which tools you will use:
- Interviews;
- Searches;
- Polygraph tests;
- Drug tests.

Select the least invasive tool that will bring you the best result. Don't *search* when *asking* will do, but don't hold back from searching when that is the best tool you have. Use tools to test the results received from other tools—searches to verify information from interviews, for example. Remember that in the end you want to have as many facts as possible and as few loose ends as possible.

"An expectation of privacy"

When it comes to probing into employee memories (interviewing), property (searches), e-mail and telephone messages, the concern is balancing the employee's right to privacy against the employer's need to know. This balancing act is a tough one but it can be made easier if the groundwork is clearly laid early in the employment relationship.

What is the necessary groundwork? Establishing that there is no right to privacy in use of employer-owned equipment, in employment-related work, in packages brought into the workplace and in workplace activities.

> **Example:** *Tyeisha sent harassing e-mail to three of her coworkers using the computer at her workspace. When one of the coworkers complained and the investigator confiscated Tyeisha's sent e-mail file, Tyeisha claimed the e-mail was her private files that no one else could see.*
>
> *Unfortunately for Tyeisha, she was wrong. Her employer provided her with a policy statement at the time she was hired explaining that anything found in an employee's computer files was discoverable by the employer, even if it had been deleted.*
>
> *Tyeisha had no privacy rights when it came to company computer files.*

An expanded discussion of privacy rights and expectations follows in the sections on searches, but the idea of balancing employee privacy rights and the employer's need to know is something to keep in mind as you think about the tools you will use to conduct you internal investigation.

Best Practices

Curbing that expectation of privacy

In addition to laws and court decisions, a key to how much privacy employees may expect is their own perception of their rights, according to Jonathan A. Segal of Philadelphia's Wolf, Block, Schorr and Solis-Cohen law firm.

In defining those perceptions, employers have the ability to destroy employees' expectations of privacy. The best way to do that is by widely distributing a clear policy that explicitly reserves the employer's right to search.

According to Segal, an employer's privacy policy should:

- Clearly articulate the items the company has the right to search:
    - Personal belongings
    - Work areas
    - Desks
    - Lockers
    - Computer documents
    - E-mail
    - Voice mail
- Explain the business reasons why a search could be necessary
    - Need to protect the workplace from illegal drugs
    - Need to protect the workplace from illegal weapons
- Set search parameters. You should search an employee, the employee's belongings or work area only when you have a reasonable suspicion that the employee has violated company policy.

Interviews

The entire next chapter is devoted to interviews but keep in mind that interviewing is your primary investigative tool. Interviews give you the opportunity to:

- Gather information about what happened;
- Find out how what happened affected the people involved;
- Find out who else has information regarding what happened;
- Find out what records and documents you need to gather;
- Find the holes in the stories that are being told to you that need filling in;
- Check the accuracy of facts provided to you;
- Obtain admissions or confessions;
- And get other information from those who saw or were involved in the conduct under investigation.

Just because interviewing a witness does not involve opening a locker, desk drawer or computer file, privacy is still an issue. Do your best to protect the privacy of information you receive and documentation witnesses provide to you. Try to select an interview location that will allow witnesses to come and go without being seen by others who do not need to know that they are being interviewed by you.

Searches

Jo-Lee from our opening example is mistaken in her assertion that the company cannot search her purse or e-mail as part of the investigation into her alleged misconduct.

Although she paid no attention to it, as part of her employee orientation, she received a handbook, part of which describes the rights reserved to the company to search personal belongings and e-mail as part of an investigation into employee misconduct. Also, much to Jo-Lee's disappointment, she skipped an employee training session on privacy rights in the workplace at which she would have revisited the rules governing searches in the workplace.

Have a business need for conducting a search. While searches are generally discouraged even when there is a legitimate business reason for having them, they are generally permitted. Business reasons include safety and internal investigations, such as allegations of employee theft.

What should you do to get this point across to employees? Establish business necessity as the employer's basis for workplace searches. The business need we are discussing in this chapter is conducting an internal investigation into a workplace conduct problem, whether that be misconduct, harassment, discrimination, unfair employment practices or some other circumstances for which an internal investigation has been convened.

> To determine if a search is fair, first ask whether the search was reasonable under the circumstances. Whether a search is reasonable depends upon the answer to the following two questions:
> 1. Was the search justified at its inception? That is, were there reasonable grounds for suspicion of work-related misconduct or was the search necessary for a non-investigative work-related purpose?
> 2. Was the search reasonable in scope? Was it carried out properly in being reasonably related to the search's objectives and not unnecessarily intrusive?

Communicate your search policy in writing to employees. Advise employees as they are hired that workplace searches are conducted. Include the policy in other employee communications, such as handbooks, newsletters and orientation.

Identify the scope of the policy. Describe all areas that are subject to be searched, such as work areas, personal files, lockers, packages, purses and backpacks, electronic files and automobiles on company property. Be sure the policy clearly states that voice mail, e-mail and the contents of the employee's desk (and work area including locker) are subject to search.

Make sure that instructions and handbooks that train employees on workplace resources, such as voice mail and e-mail, advise employees that these are provided for legitimate business use only and are subject to being reviewed/searched periodically. Describe what discipline will occur if the policy is violated.

Ensure that there are requirements and safeguards written in the policy and observed during a search. Be sure the search is conducted properly. Use trained staff to conduct the search and be sure the search is done in a professional manner.

Provide witnesses to the search. In the event the search is challenged, how will the employer prove that employee privacy rights were considered and protected? Are there witnesses to ensure that there can be no unchallenged allegation of improper conduct, such as improper touching on the part of the company representative? Maintain documentation that establishes why and how the search was conducted.

Property searches. If you can answer "yes" to the following questions before any workplace searches are conducted, you will lessen the chances that a search will be found to unlawfully invade an employee's privacy.

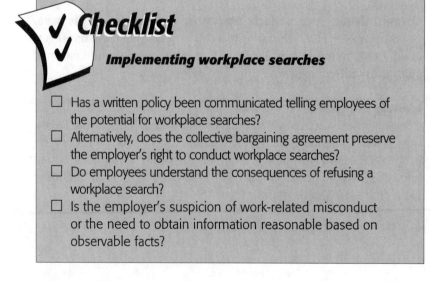

Checklist
Implementing workplace searches

- ☐ Has a written policy been communicated telling employees of the potential for workplace searches?
- ☐ Alternatively, does the collective bargaining agreement preserve the employer's right to conduct workplace searches?
- ☐ Do employees understand the consequences of refusing a workplace search?
- ☐ Is the employer's suspicion of work-related misconduct or the need to obtain information reasonable based on observable facts?

Chapter 4—The investigative tools

- ☐ Is the rationale for the search based upon violation of clearly stated work rules or the need to obtain job-critical information?
- ☐ Before the search is conducted, has an analysis been made of the employee's expectation of privacy, based upon who owns the items to be searched, how public is the area to be searched, and whether specific notice of the possibility of search was communicated?
- ☐ Is the search as limited in scope as possible, based on the nature of the investigation and the business reason for the search?
- ☐ Is any information uncovered by a search subject to strict confidentiality requirements and disseminated only on a business need to know?

Source: Jonathan A. Segal of Philadelphia's Wolf, Block, Schorr and Solis-Cohen.

Searching property is generally permitted if:
1. There is a good business reason for the search;
2. The search is conducted in a reasonable manner; and
3. The search is not discriminatory (a search of only one class of employees).

Employers that give notice that they retain the right to search personal items are more successful in defending against unlawful searches in court.

What about searching cars on the employer's property? Searches are permitted under the circumstances just listed so long as the vehicle is parked on the employer's property and is not locked. Breaking into a vehicle is not permitted as part of a search.

If an employee asks to have a lawyer, union representative or coworker present during a search of the employee's desk, locker or other personal workspace do you have to allow it? No. The right to representation only covers investigative interviews (you will learn more about this in the next chapter).

Searching desks, lockers and offices is a search of the employer's property and not the employees'. These searches are permitted at any time. But be careful not to allow employees to put their own locks on lockers, desks and company toolboxes. Doing so raises the expectation of privacy issue. Instead, provide company locks and notice indicating that there is a master key for the lock, that you retain the right to inspect the desk (or locker) at any time and that things you don't want the employer to see should not be kept in the desk (or locker).

Searching an employee. Be particularly careful when there is a need to search an employee. The first thing to remember is not to touch the employee. Rather than physically touching them, which could lead to harassment or assault charges, ask employees to empty their pockets or briefcases. If an employee refuses, insubordination charges could follow. Employers, when searching employees, also should arrange to have a witness of the same sex as the employee present. Avoid patting down or frisking employees as part of a search. Leave that to the police if needed.

Never hold the employee against his or her will. You can punish the employee for insubordination if the employee refuses your request to stay, but holding the employee is false imprisonment!

If you need to conduct a body search keep in mind that the employee may sue, and a court will require justification for the search. You will have to show:

- The search was absolutely necessary;
- There was good/reasonable cause for the body search—more than a suspicion;
- No less intrusive search would suffice; and
- The search did not go beyond what was necessary under the circumstances and was done as reasonably as possible.

Searching electronics. An employer's right to search electronic devices may be restricted by state wiretap laws and the federal Electronic Communications Privacy Act (ECPA). While an employer's right to search internal e-mail is pretty well established, the company's rights are less clear when it comes to external e-mail and voice mail.

Chapter 4—The investigative tools

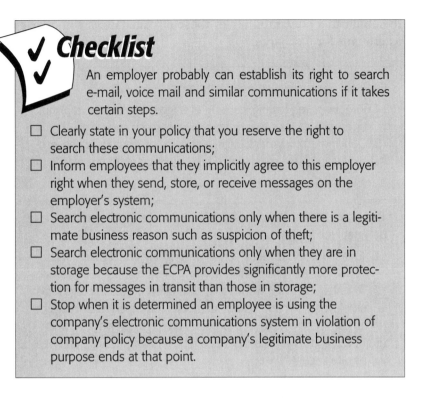

✓ Checklist

An employer probably can establish its right to search e-mail, voice mail and similar communications if it takes certain steps.

- ☐ Clearly state in your policy that you reserve the right to search these communications;
- ☐ Inform employees that they implicitly agree to this employer right when they send, store, or receive messages on the employer's system;
- ☐ Search electronic communications only when there is a legitimate business reason such as suspicion of theft;
- ☐ Search electronic communications only when they are in storage because the ECPA provides significantly more protection for messages in transit than those in storage;
- ☐ Stop when it is determined an employee is using the company's electronic communications system in violation of company policy because a company's legitimate business purpose ends at that point.

Polygraph testing

Federal law prohibits private employers from requiring, requesting, causing, or suggesting that an employee or job applicant take a lie detector test. The law defines the term "lie detector" to include a polygraph, deceptograph, voice stress analyzer, psychological stress evaluator or any other similar device (whether mechanical or electrical) that is used, or the results of which are used, for the purpose of rendering a diagnostic opinion regarding the honesty or dishonesty of an individual.

However, under limited circumstances and subject to procedural safeguards, an employer may require an employee to submit to a polygraph. If an employee is already under suspicion on the basis of independent evidence, the employee may be asked to take a polygraph as part of an ongoing investigation of economic loss, such as theft or embezzlement, to the employer's business. Assuming the employer follows the prescribed procedure, an employee's refusal to submit to a polygraph under these circumstances can be used as grounds for discharge.

Federal law prohibits an employer from:
(1) Requiring, requesting, causing or suggesting that an applicant or employee take a polygraph examination; and
(2) Denying employment to an applicant or discharging an employee because of refusal to take a polygraph or the results of a polygraph.

There are three situations in which private employers can use polygraphs:
(1) To test an employee as part of an ongoing investigation of economic loss to the employer in which the employee is a suspect,
(2) To test an applicant who would have direct access to drugs if the employer is a manufacturer, distributor, or dispenser of drugs or to test certain employees as part of an ongoing investigation, or
(3) To test certain applicants if the employer is a specifically defined private security firm.

Ongoing investigation exemption. As part of an ongoing investigation of a business loss to the employer, however, polygraph testing is permitted under these limited conditions:
(1) The investigation must involve economic loss to the employer's business;
(2) The tested employee must have had access to the missing property;
(3) The employer must have a "reasonable suspicion" that the employee to be tested was involved; and
(4) The employee must be provided with a written statement about the incident and the reasons for the employer's reasonable suspicion.

The polygraph protection law applies to all private employers with certain enumerated exceptions. Public employers are not subject to the law. Thus, government employers at the federal, state and local level can randomly test job applicants as well as existing employees. Security and pharmaceutical companies may test under certain circumstances and for particular job descriptions. Employees of national defense and security contractors of the federal government may be tested by the federal government, though not by the contractor itself.

The law sets out detailed steps that must be followed in order to give a test lawfully. For example, an employee has a right to a written statement enumerating the reasons for suspecting the employee in the incident being investigated, written notice of the date, time and location of the test, and a list of the questions asked. In addition, the law has detailed disclosure provisions that apply to the examiner as well as the employer. The extensive procedural requirements of the law mandate consulting its text prior to administering a lie detector test.

Can a tape recording device ever be considered a lie detector for purposes of the Polygraph Protection Act? One court answered this question in the affirmative, ruling that a tape recording device could be considered a lie detector within the meaning of the Act when used in conjunction with other prohibited devices to assist in the gauging of a person's truthfulness.

Many states have laws forbidding the use of polygraph tests as a condition of employment or continued employment. Federal law expressly permits states to adopt polygraph laws that are more restrictive than the federal act.

Drug testing

How does drug testing fit into a discussion about internal investigations? There may be times when a drug test will be one of the investigative tools you use. If the allegation against an employee is misconduct based on intoxication, you want to find out what the employee's workplace drug-use patterns are. Or if you are investigating a workplace accident where intoxication is suspected as a cause of the accident, the results of a blood-alcohol test will be needed.

Be very careful to know and use all of the state and federal drug-testing rules when using drug tests. While drug testing can be a useful tool, if it is not done strictly by the rules, drug testing can form the basis for an employee lawsuit.

One of the big problems with drug testing is that it may reveal drug usage that is not employment-related but part of the employee's off-duty, private life. But even if the drugs were not taken at work, their effect may be brought to work with the employee and impair the employee's ability to work at all or to work safely. Negotiating this very fine line between work-relatedness and off-duty conduct is difficult. That is one of the reasons why taking great care when using drug testing and when deciding to use drug testing is essential.

Worst case scenario

His supervisor has alleged that "Ace" (Joseph on his employment record) was drinking beer while at work. He was sent home once and suspended twice for being high on the job. Ace claimed all three times that he was not drunk or drinking.

Before terminating Ace, you conduct an internal investigation. Everyone you interview describes erratic behavior on Ace's part. A few say they think he drinks on the job. However, no one says they have ever seen him drinking at work.

You fire him, based on what the witnesses have said. Two weeks later you find out that the company is being sued by "Ace" for wrongful termination. Ace wins the lawsuit and steep damages. Why? It ends up he is a diabetic and the times he was "acting erratically" had to do with his insulin regulation.

Solution: When the allegation of misconduct is based on being intoxicated at work, request a drug test to confirm or disprove that the employee was intoxicated. It is one of the tools in your investigation arsenal not to be abused or used lightly. But you may use it when appropriate for determining whether alcohol is a factor in an allegation.

You may conclude that an employee is under the influence of drugs or alcohol by observing the employee's behavior. You might:
- Smell alcohol on the employee's breath;
- Observe slurred speech;
- Observe unsteady walking;
- Notice clumsy movement; or
- See overt disorientation.

In addition, you may find evidence of drug or alcohol use, such as drug paraphernalia or empty alcohol bottles in:
- Vehicles;
- Lockers;
- Tool boxes;
- Lunch boxes; or
- Purses or backpacks.

Remember that the same set of symptoms could be related to an illness or prescribed medication. Tell the employee what you suspect. Ask what's going on and require verification of any medial explanation given. If no medical explanation is given and you have a drug-testing policy, follow through with your procedure and include the results of the test in your investigation information.

Be careful in making an accusation of drug or alcohol use based on observation of odd behavior alone, warns Robert E. Gregg of the law firm of Boardman, Suhr, Curry & Field LLP (Madison, Wisconsin). Observation is not enough. "Spacey" behavior can also be a symptom of illness and you cannot immediately know which behavior is intoxication and which is the early phase of a stroke or a diabetic condition.

Instead of telling an employee to go home when you observe erratic behavior, seek medical attention or send the employee home in the care of a family member who can get them help. The first concern should be for employee safety, not employee discipline, advises Gregg.

The Quiz

1. There are searches that an employer may conduct without calling in law enforcement. ❑ True ❑ False

2. If behavior is the result of prescribed medication, request verification of the medical condition. ❑ True ❑ False

3. Always make employees feel confident that they have an expectation of privacy in employer-owned computers. ❑ True ❑ False

4. Instead of patting an employee down, ask him or her to empty his or her pockets. ❑ True ❑ False

5. Which of these is not an investigative tool:
   a. Interviewing.
   b. Forcefully detaining the employee.
   c. Polygraph testing.
   d. Computer search.

Answer key: 1. T; 2. T; 3. F; 4. T; 5. b.

Chap 5

The Interviews

Interviewing dos and don'ts	74
Allowing employee representatives to sit in	76
Handling refusals to be interviewed	79
Location, location, location	80
Interviewing tips	82
BEST PRACTICES: Model interview	88
How to ask good questions	90
Taking notes	92
The Quiz	93

On numerous occasions, Tina told her boss, Eytan, that she did not want to go out with him and that she'd take her chances of not being promoted before she'd have an affair with him.

Now Tina has filed a sexual harassment complaint and Laila, a member of your HR staff, has been selected as the investigator. Laila has had training as a sexual harassment investigator and has an outline to follow for planning her investigation.

In addition to Tina and Eytan, Laila has identified six other witnesses whom she will interview. Before her first interview, which is scheduled for tomorrow, Laila wants to spend an afternoon learning a bit about each of the parties to the complaint, Tina and Eytan, and the witnesses. Having done that, she will be ready to begin interviewing in the morning. How should Laila conduct her interviews? In what order? What types of questions should she ask?

Interviewing dos and don'ts

We already know that the investigator must be someone who can communicate well with a variety of different personality types and across ethnic, gender and racial boundaries. Why? Because if the investigator cannot conduct a good interview, there is little or no chance that the investigation will succeed in resolving the issues raised in any complaint brought for internal investigation.

The following checklist will help you formulate guidelines for conducting interviews that are fair, productive and focused on the investigation at hand.

✓ Checklist

Interviewing dos and don'ts

- ☐ Do remember that participation is voluntary
- ☐ Don't reveal what you already know
- ☐ Do watch for leading questions
- ☐ Do use open-ended & specific questions
- ☐ Do interview all relevant people—don't stop with the complainant & the accused. Include nonemployees where applicable
- ☐ Do know something about the person you are going to interview and craft your questions for them
- ☐ Do observe body language, but don't overanalyze
- ☐ Don't play judge—always treat the accused as innocent
- ☐ Don't wander—stick to the scope of the investigation
- ☐ Do plan on having follow-up interviews
- ☐ Don't forget these: Privacy & Confidentiality

As you begin the interview process, keep in mind that participation in an investigation is voluntary—you want cooperation, but you cannot force it. Tell the interviewee that you would like cooperation, and emphasize the need for confidentiality—both on your part as the investigator and on the part of the witness. Always make the interviewee comfortable.

Conduct an initial interview, then bring the person back later in the day to review your summary of the interview. The review will give the person an opportunity to recall additional details that may help you in your investigation.

Who gets interviewed first?
Unless you have a good reason to vary, generally:
Start with the person bringing the complaint. Find out all of his or her allegations before moving on. You will need that information to plan the specifics of the rest of your investigation.

Next, interview the person being accused of harassment or discrimination or unfair conduct. Interviewing the accused before other witnesses helps reinforce the objectivity of the investigation—fewer preconceived notions. If you are lucky, the accused may admit to some or all of the allegations, making the investigation process easier.

Finally, interview all other witnesses—include nonemployees when they have information to add to your investigation.

Use the information obtained from the complainant and the accused to locate other witnesses to interview.

Always begin by explaining what the investigation is about (its focus) and why the witness has been summoned for an interview.

Observe body language but don't overinterpret. Your role is not to psychoanalyze the witness but to find out what the witness knows. Use "congruent communication" to be sure you don't misinterpret. What's "congruent communication"? A way to discover a witness's real meaning, by evaluating the:

◆ Words (10%);
◆ Voice tone (40%); and
◆ Body language (50%).

Remember to treat the accused as innocent throughout the entire investigation. An employee is "innocent until proven guilty."

> For each person you interview:
>
> **Review the scope of the investigation.** Spell out the subject matter at the beginning of each interview.
>
> **Ask for leads.** Ask each interviewee if they are aware of any other witnesses. Ask each interviewee if there is any relevant information or evidence that you may be missing.
>
> **Provide an opportunity to give input.** Give each interviewee an open-ended chance to speak on any relevant topic.
>
> **Take notes.** Take good, detailed notes during the interview. Avoid tape recorders because they may cause interviewees to become unnecessarily guarded.
>
> **Get a "sign off."** After each interview, have the employee "sign off" on the notes you have taken. Give them a chance to scribble in their own notations if they wish to comment on or add to your notes.

Allowing employee representatives to sit in

Union reps. Union employees who are accused of misconduct have the right to request the presence of a union representative at an investigatory interview that could result in discipline. The National Labor Relations Board (NLRB) has also extended this right to nonunion employees who are accused of misconduct—they have the right to have a coworker present at an investigatory interview.

Weingarten rights to representation

Unionized employees who are accused of misconduct have the right to representation in investigative interviews with their employers according to the 1975 US Supreme Court decision in *NLRB v Weingarten* (420 US 25). The court's decision did not address whether a nonunion employee has the same right.

In July of 2000, the NLRB determined that nonunion employees do have the same right to representation in discipline actions against them.

What does the extended Weingarten rule allow? If an investigative interview may reasonably be expected to result in disciplinary action, a union or nonunion employee who is covered by the National

tional Labor Relations Act (NLRA) may request to have a coworker present during the interview.

Who is covered by the NLRA? Most public sector employees are covered by the NLRA. This includes employees of nonprofit organizations such as private schools, private universities, hospitals and charities.

The NLRA does not cover:
- Small employers;
- Government agencies;
- Employees in the airlines or railroad industries who are covered by the Railway Labor Act;
- Some specialized industries (horse racing and dog racing, for example); and
- Supervisors and independent contractors.

If an employee is not covered by the NLRA, check to see if some other civil service or organization rule gives the employee the right to representation during an investigative interview into an allegation of misconduct by the employee.

Weingarten rights are not like *Miranda* rights that must be given before someone is interviewed. You are not required to inform the person of his or her rights under *Weingarten* before conducting an interview.

What if the accused asks for representation once the interview has begun? You have three choices in this situation:
1. Stop the interview until the representative arrives;
2. Call off the interview and reschedule for a time when the representative is present; or
3. Give the employee a choice of calling off the interview or giving up his or her right to have representation or a coworker present—this would result in your taking the disciplinary action without hearing the employee's side of the story and is not a good option.

What is a coworker's role in an investigative interview? The coworker may make a statement in support of the accused employee and may ask for clarification of a question or of confusing or intimidating tactics. The coworker may not, however, purposely disrupt the interview without a good reason.

Keep in mind that coworker representation is only required during an *investigative interview*. If you are simply informing the employee of the disciplinary action you will take, requests for representation need not be honored.

> **DON'T miss this**
>
> *Investigatory interviews are those in which an employee is investigated or questioned or when the employee reasonably fears that some sort of discipline may result.*

"Lawyering up." What if the witness wants a lawyer present? An employee is not entitled to attorney representation during investigatory interviews unless the employee is the accused and there is a collective bargaining agreement or civil service rule that provides for representation, or unless criminal allegations are made or surface.

On the other hand, if the accused wants to have an attorney present, consider allowing it. Your gesture will reinforce the neutrality of the interview and investigation. In addition, if the investigation is looking into employee misconduct, the attorney may see that the evidence against the employee is strong and advise the employee against suing the employer later on.

In deciding whether to agree with an accused employee's request to have his or her attorney present during an interview, consult with your organization's legal counsel before making your decision.

If it is agreed that an attorney will be present, do not allow the attorney to object or otherwise interrupt the interview. Politely, but firmly indicate to the accused and the attorney that the attorney is there as an observer only!

WHAT you need to know

If an accused asks for representation and does not have a legal right to it, as described above, reassure him or her that:
- No conclusions have been reached;
- The investigations will be conducted fairly and objectively; and
- Confidentiality will be maintained to the fullest extent.

It is possible that the accused still might have legitimate concerns about the integrity of the process. If so, these concerns should be addressed immediately.

Chapter 5—The interviews 79

Friends or family members. And if the accused asks to have a friend or family member present during an investigative interview, do you have to allow it? No. The rule only states a coworker's presence may be requested, not a friend or family member. However, check your collective bargaining agreements and organization policies. There might be a provision in one of those documents that does allow for a friend or family member to be with an accused in an investigative interview.

The complainant. There are no NLRB rules governing requests by complainants for representation (by a lawyer, union rep or coworker) during an investigative interview. If you receive this type of request, consult with your organization's legal counsel before making a decision.

If representation (by a lawyer, union rep or coworker) would make the complainant feel more comfortable while being interviewed, consider allowing it.

Handling refusals to be interviewed

Zena is someone you would like to interview in your investigation of Tina's harassment complaint against Eytan. Unfortunately, she has flatly refused your requests for an interview. What do you do?

As we learned at the beginning of this chapter, witness participation in an internal investigation is voluntary. Explain to all potential witnesses that you would like cooperation, and emphasize that you will respect the need for confidentiality to the extent it is possible.

- ◆ **When the accused refuses to be interviewed.** The accused needs to know that you want to hear both sides of the story before drawing any conclusions. But firmly make it clear that if the accused refuses to talk to you, you will complete your investigation without his or her input. You may be able to discipline the employee, but that will not help your investigation.

- **When the alleged victim refuses to be interviewed.** Again, you cannot compel the person to be interviewed and you may discipline him or her—but to what end? This situation arises most often when an employee informs the employer that a coworker is being harassed, but that person does not want to do anything about it. Or when a complainant doesn't want to follow through with a complaint once it is filed. If the refusal is absolute—the person cannot be convinced to be interviewed—continue the investigation with the information you are able to gather. You may still be able to stop someone's harassing or discriminating practices.

> Public employees cannot be forced to be witnesses against themselves.
>
> A special rule (the *Garrity* rule) applies to public employees who are accused of misconduct that may later be the basis for a criminal prosecution.
>
> If the public employee invokes his or her protections under the Fifth Amendment to the Constitution and refuses to give information that may be used to incriminate him or her in a criminal prosecution, the employer cannot threaten to fire the employee for not cooperating ("If you won't testify, you're fired!").
>
> If the employer wants to compel the testimony, the employee must be given immunity from future prosecution.

Location, location, location

While these three words—location, location, location—usually form the mantra of real estate talk, where you conduct your interview is also an important locational decision. You want to find a place where your interview and how long it takes are not open for all to see. First of all, you want whoever you are interviewing to be concentrating on your discussion and not on people walking by but, more importantly, you want the person you are interviewing to feel free to speak without being seen or overheard. While it may not always be the case, some interviewees will be providing you with sensitive or confidential information. The process of obtaining that information must be protected by privacy.

Chapter 5—The interviews

Worst case scenario

Laila is now ready to begin her interview with Eytan, the man who is accused of sexually harassing Tina. There has been some whispered gossip about Tina filing a harassment claim, but no one knows yet who the accused is.

Laila uses the conference room in your building. Unfortunately, that conference room is located in the frequently traveled hallway between two sections of the facility. It is also glass-walled, although it is soundproof.

It is also well known in the office that Laila is the person charged with investigating sexual harassment complaints. Within minutes of Eytan's walking into the room for his interview with Laila, the entire floor is abuzz with the news that Eytan got caught sexually harassing Tina. It won't take long for the rumor to get back to him—whether he is found to have harassed Tina or not!

Solution: If this is the only conference room available and there is no private office in the building to be used for the interview, Laila should consider using an office or conference room in another of your facilities or renting one in another facility. Preserving the privacy and confidentiality of an investigative interview is of utmost importance and should always be a primary concern.

To the extent possible, who you are interviewing should not be known to others. If privacy or anonymity cannot be found at your facility, consider another location that has a conference room or private office.

WHAT you need to know

In this day and age the question will arise: can interviews be conducted by telephone? The answer is a qualified no! Interviews should be conducted face-to-face. At a minimum, your interview with any complainant or accused should be conducted in person. If absolutely necessary, an interview with a "minor" witness could be over the phone.

Interviewing tips

Let's go back to the opening scenario and see what the interview that Laila conducts looks like. Remember, in this example we're assuming that Tina brought a sexual harassment complaint against Eytan and Laila has been asked to serve as investigator.

Interviewing the complainant

The following are some tips on interviewing the complaining employee ("the complainant") once an investigation into workplace harassment has begun. These tips are applicable either during the initial meeting or in a follow-up meeting once an investigator has been assigned.

1. **Get details.** Ask the employee for specific details regarding the alleged workplace harassment. Include questions regarding:
   ◆ The type of conduct and its frequency;
   ◆ What was said or done;
   ◆ Where it occurred;
   ◆ The dates that the conduct occurred; and
   ◆ The time period over which the conduct occurred.

   Find out whether or not there was a pattern of previous episodes; was the person bringing the complaint aware of similar behavior by the accused towards any other employee?

2. **Understand the context.** Get the specific context in which the conduct occurred, including the nature and general description of the work area and the specific location.

   Find out whether the conduct occurred at a work-related function, during working time, or after hours. Also determine the time relationship between the occurrence of the alleged conduct, its effect on the complainant, and the time when the complainant made the report. If there was a time lag between the occurrence and the report, find out why the complainant waited before reporting the situation. A plausible explanation may be the employee's fear, either of retaliation or simple embarrassment.

   It is helpful to prepare a detailed chronology. This will help you analyze whether there might have been certain events that triggered the complaint—for example, a denial of promotion, pay raise or a transfer.

Find out if there are any witnesses or documents that may support the claim. For example, ask about cards, letters, notes, voice mail messages, e-mail messages, expense reports, diaries, pictures or photographs.

3. **Understand the impact.** Determine the effect of the conduct on the complainant.
   ◆ Identify what harm the conduct caused. For example, were there financial or economic effects?
   ◆ Did the complainant miss work or visit the doctor?
   ◆ What about psychological effects like sleeplessness, loss of appetite, depression or anxiety?
   ◆ Was the conduct received as a joke?
   ◆ Was it really unwelcome?
   ◆ Did it embarrass, frighten or humiliate the complainant?

   Often, employees state that, while they may have acted as if they were not offended by harassment, they did so out of fear or because they felt threatened or intimidated. It is important to remember that the real issue is whether the behavior was unwelcome. Probe gently to get as much information as possible.

4. **Find out what the complainant wants.** Try to find out how the employee wants the situation resolved. It may be hard for him or her to come up with a succinct answer; in fact, it's possible that the complainant has never considered that question. Probe further by finding out:
   ◆ Can the employee continue to work for or with the accused?
   ◆ Can the employee be productive?
   ◆ Will it be embarrassing or awkward for the employee, enough so that it will interfere with the employee's ability to do the job?
   ◆ Does the employee need counseling?

5. **Explain the next steps.** Explain that the charges are serious and that the organization will conduct a thorough investigation before reaching any conclusions. Assure the employee that he or she will not be retaliated against for making the complaint—regardless of the outcome.

Make no statements about the accused's character, job performance or family life, either to excuse or condemn the alleged behavior. If the accused were to sue for defamation, this might be enough evidence for a finding of "malice" or spitefulness. Malice wipes out the legal privilege that employers have to lawfully discuss these kinds of situations internally.

6. **Get a written statement.** Ask the employee to provide the details of the complaint in writing. If the employee is reluctant to write it down, don't argue, but make a note of the employee's reluctance. If the employee agrees to provide a written summary, attorney Lisa Lavelle Burke suggests that it include:
   - A list of all the employee's issues, concerns and complaints;
   - The relevant facts and dates the employee believes support his or her concerns;
   - The names of people the employee thinks may have information relevant to the investigation; and
   - Suggestions for obtaining relevant documentation (such as memos or performance reviews).

7. **Summarize.** Burke, speaking at a seminar cosponsored by Patton Boggs, LLP, CCH INCORPORATED and the Society for Human Resource Management (SHRM), also suggested providing a memo or letter to the employee summarizing the issues raised. This document will provide both the organization and the complaining employee an opportunity to make sure that all of the issues are clearly understood and that nothing has been left out.
The confirmation memo should:
   - Identify the issues;
   - Identify the facts provided by the employee to support the issues;
   - Confirm these are all the issues raised;
   - Identify the person investigating the matter and confirm his or her impartiality and fairness;
   - Identify a roadmap for the investigation; and
   - Outline the employer's expectations for the employee raising the issue.

Interviewing the accused

Once HR has met with the person who brought the complaint, it is time to meet with the person accused of inappropriate conduct ("the accused"). If there is more than one person who is accused, meet with each one individually rather than together.

1. **Explain the reason for the meeting.** Begin by telling the accused the purpose of the investigation. He or she may have no idea why the meeting was called. Provide enough information about the complaint so that the accused can know what he or she is responding to. Explain that a full, thorough investigation of the allegations will be conducted before any conclusions are reached. Assure the accused that confidentiality will be maintained to the fullest extent. Explain that disclosure of information about the complaint and investigation will be strictly limited to those with a legitimate need to know.

    It is important that HR treat the accused party with respect and objectivity. Do not make assumptions about guilt based on prior history or simply on the fact that a complaint has been made. Conduct a complete investigation of the current situation.

2. **Obtain a statement.** As with the complainant, ask the accused for a written statement. HR usually has more leverage with the accused than with the complainant because of the potential disciplinary nature of the investigation. Again, if the accused refuses to provide a written statement, document that fact.

3. **Identify the accused's relationship to the complainant.** Was the accused a supervisory employee, a coworker or a nonemployee? If the individual was a supervisor, indicate the individual's job title, obtain a copy of the individual's job description, and determine the individual's specific duties at the time of the alleged harassment.

    Determine whether the accused directed, or had responsibility for, the work of the complainant or other employees.
    - ◆ Did he or she have authority to recommend employment decisions affecting others (for example, hiring, firing or promoting)?
    - ◆ Was he or she responsible for maintaining or administering the records of others?

- If sexual harassment is alleged, was there any prior consensual relationship between the parties?
- How long have the parties known each other?
- Is there a history of group or individual socializing?
- Is there a motive for the complainant to make false charges?

Note that the employer is liable for the actions of supervisory employees or agents with immediate or successively higher authority over the victim, regardless of whether the acts were authorized or even forbidden by the employer, and regardless of whether the employer knew or should have known of their occurrence.

Consider how the accused reacts. You can expect the accused to deny the charges. Observe the reaction. Note whether or not there is surprise, anger or disbelief.

Describe the details of the complaint and pay attention to the areas of disagreement between each person's recollection of the events. If the accused denies the allegations, probe further to determine what he or she thinks are the reasons that could have motivated the employee to make the complaint. Determine if there are any facts to support the accused's side of the story.

If the person accused of harassment does not deny the conduct but explains the circumstances, there may be no need to investigate further. In this case, determine an appropriate response.

4. **Gather more evidence.** Find out if there are any witnesses, documentation or other evidence that can support the accused's denial of the allegations. When faced with a "he said, she said" claim, investigate further. If there are no witnesses to the alleged conduct, ask other employees if they have ever been subject to objectionable conduct, but do not name the accused.

In addition to liability to harassment victims, employers could also be liable to harassers for inadequate or incomplete investigations. When employment decisions are based on workplace harassment investigations, good investigative practices must be used.

5. **Caution against wrongdoing.** Warn the accused that retaliation against the complainant is prohibited and can result in discipline, up to and including discharge. Caution the accused of the risk of personal defamation liability if he or she makes malicious or false statements or discusses the matter with others. It's important to stress these things in every case regardless of your personal belief as to whether or not the complaint was legitimate.

Interviewing other witnesses

Interview anyone who has knowledge that will support or deny the complainant's allegations—employees and nonemployees. If possible, obtain signed statements. Witness evidence is very critical to the investigation. Without it, it is simply the complainant's word against that of the accused. Determine whether information provided by witnesses is based on firsthand knowledge of the facts, hearsay or gossip. And document unsuccessful attempts to interview persons who no longer work for the organization.

Be aware that often witnesses are reluctant to come forward out of fear of punishment or even of awkwardness among their fellow employees. Assure witnesses that their cooperation is important, that their testimony is confidential and that they will not be retaliated against for providing honest responses and information. Warn witnesses of the risk of personal defamation liability if they make malicious or false statements or discuss the matter with others.

Don't unnecessarily disclose information to witnesses. For example, instead of asking, "Did you see Eytan touch Tina?" ask "Have you seen anyone touch Tina at work in a way that made her feel uncomfortable?"

🏅 Best Practices

Model interview

How will you actually conduct your interview? What will you ask and say? Michael Johnson, J.D. and Andrew Fosse, J.D. suggest the following model for interviewing:

Prepare an outline of topics—You don't need to write out the questions verbatim.

Identify the topics you need to address with each witness. Ask yourself:

- What has the complainant alleged happened? What is in dispute?
- What laws or employment polices may have been broken?
- What relevant information might this witness possess?
- Don't be wedded to your outline. You may have to jump around.

Structure the interview

- Introduce yourself.
- Inform witness of the purpose of the interview.
- Stress that no conclusions have been reached. The goal is to try to hear all sides of the story.
- Try to put the witness at ease.

A friendly, conversational approach usually works better than an aggressive cross-examination. You're very unlikely to get the accused to admit to the misconduct or get the complainant to admit that he or she made it all up. You want the witnesses to talk as much as possible so that you can obtain as much information as possible, look for inconsistencies in the witnesses' stories, and make your own credibility determinations. However, don't be afraid to ask the tough questions.

If the witness is not cooperating fully, politely but persistently seek an answer to your questions.

Compile an employment history with the organization. Questions about the witness's employment history with the organization are easy questions that get the witness talking and help you establish a rapport.

These questions also communicate to the witness how the interview is going to work. That is, you will ask a question, the witness will answer the question, you will pause and write down the answer, and then you will ask the next question.

It is important to write down the answers given to these questions, even though you probably already have this information recorded elsewhere. If you don't take notes on the answers given until the witness gives you an important piece of information, you may tip off the witness that he or she just made an important statement. The witness may then try to "clarify" the answer given.

Because witnesses are very unlikely to lie about their employment history, observing the witness's body language and demeanor can set a baseline for contrasting the witness's body language and demeanor when providing answers that you believe are untruthful.

Questions about the matter under investigation. As a general rule, address nonthreatening topics first and hard topics last.

Closing litany. Always end up by asking: "Is there anything else that we have not discussed that you think is relevant to this matter?"

Ask the employee or witness to contact you if he or she later thinks of additional information or documents that may be relevant. Also ask:
- Who else should we interview?
- Are there any documents relating to this issue? (Define what you mean by documents.)
- Remind employee that retaliation is illegal.
- Explain to employee that you will limit your discussions of the information he or she provided to those with a legitimate reason to know about the matter only.

> Request that the employee keep the matter confidential. Tell the employee that keeping the matter confidential protects the integrity of the investigation and protects the witness from a defamation lawsuit.
>
> Thank the person for his or her cooperation.

Source: Brightline Compliance, LLC (2003).

How to ask good questions

- Use fact-finding questioning techniques to find out how, what, when, where, and who they know.
- Use open-ended questions. Use words like describe, explain, tell me about...
- Exhaust the topic before moving on. Ask, What else? Anything else? Always? Is that all?
- Follow up. Once the witness has answered your open-ended question, follow up by asking about each incident, event or conversation revealed separately.
- Probe into nonresponsive answers. If the interviewee says, "I don't recall," ask what that means. "Does that mean that you don't remember but it could have happened or if it had happened you would recall?"
- Ask the person to fill in any gaps. "What about ... ?" "Were there times that ... ?"
- Look for corroboration: Who else was there? Who else knows about this? Did you tell anyone what happened? When? Who?
- Don't reveal what you know. The interviewee will probably assume you know more than you do and will tell you all he or she knows, which may be more than you do know.
- Use a combination of open-ended (questions that call for a narrative) and specific questions to get information, and then close in on an answer.
- Do not ask leading questions.

What is a *leading question*? One that presumes an answer or information about the answer you are looking for. "Is it true that you worked late on January 10, 2003?" is a leading question. Instead ask whether the person has ever worked late or what the person did on January 10, 2003, and let him or her tell you what he or she did.

In an interview, it is better to ask open-ended, narrative questions, that is, questions that allow the person to tell you what happened, rather than confirming what you already think you know with a yes or no answer.

- Don't interrupt the witness while he or she is answering your questions. Instead, make notes and ask another question.
- Before you ask a question, it is useful to set it up.

Next I'd like to find out about the events on the day that Deter first made unwelcomed advances to you. Instead of just asking what happened, build up to that question:
- *Where were you?*
- *When were you there?*
- *Who else was there?*
- *What happened?*

Setting up the question helps the witness go back in time and visualize what happened. It also makes sure that you ask about anyone else who was there and might have information.

Be sure to listen to each answer. Don't get so caught up thinking about your next question that you forget to listen to what the witness is saying.

Johnson and Foose, quoted above, advise interviewers to avoid certain types of questions:
- Avoid questions that call for a legal conclusion;
- Avoid compound questions ("Did you do thus-and-such, and if so, when and how?");
- Avoid legalese—use simple, direct language;

- Avoid beginning a question with "Do you recall…?" It allows the witness to simply answer yes or no and not give any further information;
- Don't encourage hearsay or personal opinions, but if they are offered during an interview, use them as jumping off points for other questions or additional witnesses or documents;

> Johnson and Foose define hearsay as evidence based on the report of others, rather than the personal knowledge of a witness.
>
> For example, "Did you hear Alec asking Liane for a date?" "No, but she said he did," is hearsay.
>
> Although hearsay is generally not admissible in court, it is acceptable in an investigative interview. Just don't base your conclusion on hearsay, Johnson and Foose warn.

- Finally, avoid being interviewed by the interviewee. Be polite, but firm in refusing to say who else you are interviewing or have interviewed. Explain that you are not free to disclose that information, just as you would not disclose that you talked to this witness, but that if the person knows of people he or she thinks should be interviewed you would appreciate that information to help make your investigation complete. Likewise, don't disclose what you have already learned or what you hope to find out. You ask the questions! Your control the interview!

Taking notes

You will come into the interview with written questions you want to ask the witness. Explain to the witness that you have notes you will be referring to and that you will be taking notes during the interview. Assure the person that you will ask him or her to review the notes after you have gone over them and put them in order. Ask if the witness has any questions or concerns about the notes and clear those up before proceeding with the interview.

Recognize that your note-taking may make some witnesses uncomfortable. Do what you can to ease that discomfort.

Chapter 5—The interviews

It is a good idea to have two columns on your note paper. One with the questions you want to ask and one alongside that for the answers that are given. Have a separate pad or paper to jot down additional questions that come up as the interview progresses.

Make a check mark or other indication that you've asked a question. This will help you to know which questions still need asking.

Take a moment at the end of the interview to look over your notes. Check for any questions that you missed or any new questions that came up but you forgot to ask.

WHAT you need to know

> Should you tape record interviews?
>
> There is no rule against tape recording interviews, and there are different schools of thought on its effectiveness and its potential chilling affect, but personal handwritten notes are preferable.
>
> If you do tape interviews, make sure that the first thing on the tape is a recording of the witness's consent to be taped.

The Quiz

1. You only want to interview employees during an internal investigation. ❑ True ❑ False

2. Which order is best for setting up your interview schedule:
   a. Accused, complainant, other witnesses.
   b. Complainant, other witnesses, accused.
   c. Complainant, accused, other witnesses.

3. In all cases select a location for an internal investigation that is in the facility where the event being investigated took place. ❑ True ❑ False

4. You must have a warrant to tape record an internal investigation. ❑ True ❑ False

Continued on next page

Continued from previous page

5. If a witness refuses to be interviewed you should:
   a. Take the witness to court and have a judge compel him or her to provide information.
   b. Remind the witness that his or her cooperation is mandatory.
   c. Dismiss the witness at the first sign of a lack of cooperation.
   d. None of the above.

Answer key: 1. F; 2. c; 3. F; 4. F; 5. d.

Chapter 6

Document, document, document

Why is it important to document?... 96
Use the law firm of Who, What, Where, When, Why & How........ 97
Take clear, detailed notes—leave your tape recorder at home....... 101
Get a "sign off" from each interview.. 102
Final review.. 103
Document retention 103
The Quiz... 108

> *HR has received several complaints about Barbara, a line-manager, from a group of employees who work under her. The complaints allege that Barbara has repeatedly made rude, offensive comments regarding certain employees whom she supervises. Recognizing that the employer has a duty to investigate such complaints, your supervisor has instructed you to investigate the situation. Your supervisor has cautioned you, however, that while investigating this situation, you must be able to avoid, or at least mitigate to the greatest extent possible, any legal liability your employer could incur as a result of the investigation. Specifically, your supervisor has told you to be careful in collecting and creating documentation regarding the investigation. What do you need to know about such documentation?*

Why is it important to document?

Memories may fade, but documents will be there to tell the story of your investigation. It is crucial that HR record what was said during the investigation and what was done in response. Documentation is important to ensure that, down the road, other HR staff members are able to acquire the knowledge of the investigation.

Documentation also provides a record that supports and substantiates actions taken during, and as a result of, the investigation, thereby making personnel decisions less subject to legal challenge and, when challenged, easier to defend. It can be invaluable in defending against a wrongful discharge, defamation, sexual harassment or other type of lawsuit. If an organization's documentation is not timely, accurate and written, the organization may lose in court. The employer's documents are often at the heart of such disputes.

Always document your investigative activities, noting the date, time, place and your remarks about the incident. Throughout the investigation, repeatedly ask those involved whether or not they have any documentation that would be helpful in the investigation. And document their responses! A complete and accurate record can show that an employer promptly and thoroughly investigated a complaint and that its resolution of the complaint was appropriate. Also, it can be invaluable in defending against a wrongful discharge or defamation lawsuit by a person found guilty of misconduct.

Timing is everything

To ensure accuracy, documentation should be created as soon as possible. Since memory tends to be less accurate as time goes by, timely documentation helps ensure the most accurate documentation possible.

Date every document. It sounds like something that should not have to be said. However, it is not uncommon to find personnel files loaded with documentation that has not been dated. Often the absence of a date renders a document useless. Dating all documentation is important. Dates are also important to help refresh the memory of the individual who wrote them. By arranging the documentation chronologically, a pattern can be quickly and easily ascertained.

Past documentation. In conducting an investigation, prior misconduct, if any, should be addressed, but only when that misconduct has been documented and is relevant to the investigation at hand. If prior misconduct was not documented at the time, even if it is known by you to have occurred, then it probably should not be used in a subsequent situation.

Likewise, if the prior documentation has no meaning or impact to the current investigation, it is not appropriate to automatically include the information. Each situation requires objective review and judgment.

Use the law firm of Who, What, Where, When, Why & How

Knowing how to create good documentation isn't an inborn trait that comes with being put in charge of an investigation. Every organization has its own documentation format and procedures, but there are common elements that are found in all good documentation.

What to include

What should you include in documentation to make it meaningful, helpful or useful? The thought process for creating good documentation is similar to that used by news reporters—tell the whole story in an objective manner. Journalists are taught to look at the following:

- **Who** was involved in the incident/misconduct? Who witnessed it? Who is administering discipline?
- **What** behavior is causing the problem? What can be done to correct it? What behavior is expected in the future? What are the consequences for engaging in the undesired behavior?
- **Where** did the incident/misconduct take place?
- **When** did the incident/misconduct take place? Using a time line may help place the facts in context.
- **Why** is the behavior inappropriate? Why is discipline warranted (or unwarranted)?
- **How** did the incident/misconduct occur? How did the incident/misconduct impact your business?

DON'T miss this

Documenting how the incident/misconduct impacted your business is cited by decision makers as the key to effective documentation as it shows what your legitimate business reason was for the action taken.

✓ Checklist

What do I need to document?

☐ **Reason(s) for the investigation.** Document the reason(s) why the investigation is being conducted. If the investigation is based on a complaint, obtain a written statement from the person making the complaint if possible. In situations where the person making the complaint is not willing to write or sign a complaint, then you should prepare a written summary of the complaint and make an effort to have the person who made the complaint confirm that the contents of the written summary are accurate.

☐ **Witness' statements.** Employees who are interviewed should be asked to sign the interview summary, sign an acknowledgement or write their own version of the event. Save all written statements submitted by the person making the complaint, the accused and witnesses, as well as any other documentation or materials acquired during the investigation. For information on conducting effective interviews, see Chapter 5.

☐ **Other evidence relevant to the investigation.** Such documents might include:
 ☐ Agenda/itineraries;
 ☐ Collective bargaining agreements;
 ☐ Computer files—even "deleted" computer files may possibly be recovered by an expert;
 ☐ E-mail messages;
 ☐ Employee handbooks;
 ☐ Expense reports;
 ☐ Logs;

- ☐ Past documentation relevant to the event—attach past warnings, incident reports and performance appraisals, as applicable;
- ☐ Personnel files;
- ☐ Posted information and other communications to employees;
- ☐ Receipts;
- ☐ Relevant policies and procedures;
- ☐ Samples of work;
- ☐ Security records;
- ☐ Supervisors' notes;
- ☐ Time records;
- ☐ Training records;
- ☐ Travel documents; and
- ☐ Written memoranda.

☐ **Course of the investigation.** Document the original written plan of who will be interviewed and list the topics to be addressed in the interviews. Document any changes in the course of the investigation and why those changes occurred.

☐ **Investigative findings.** Document a summary of the investigative findings and the conclusions drawn.

☐ **Action taken as a result of the investigation.** Document any actions taken as a result of the investigation as well as the reasons those actions were taken. If no action is taken, document the reasons why.

☐ **Action plan for follow up.** Document your action plan to follow-up on the actions taken as a result of the investigation.

☐ **Signature and dates.** Employees who are interviewed should be asked to sign the interview summary, sign an acknowledgement or write their own version of the event. If the employee refuses to sign, make a note on the document and have a witness sign the note.

WHAT you need to know

Assume that all documents are "discoverable" if a lawsuit is filed. This means that, unless the document is protected by the attorney-client privilege, the opposing side will have access to it. You should be prepared to have the person who is the subject of the investigation and his/her attorney scrutinize every document generated during the investigation.

Be careful not to disclose privileged or otherwise confidential material to people outside the scope of the privilege; otherwise you will waive the privilege. Clarify with your attorney who in the organization can have access to the documents or information. Give or show documents only to those people who must see them in order to take personnel actions or if absolutely necessary to obtain information essential to the investigation. If copies are given out, make sure that each and every copy is returned to the investigator for destruction. Generally, the fewer individuals who have access to disciplinary documentation, the better.

Document communications with all employees

Consistency is critical with respect to documentation. Similar job-related communications should be documented for all employees, including both positive and negative comments and occurrences. The documentation process should *not* be used to build a case against one employee if other employees in similar situations did not have their actions documented. Inconsistent documentation could be used as proof that a person was chosen for discharge or other adverse employment actions for unlawful reasons.

When a situation is not documented consistently, the organization may not be able to defend itself if faced with a grievance, complaint or litigation. The lack of documentation might be used, for example, to show discriminatory intent, to show that the organization doesn't have employee relations programs, or to show that the organization acted in an arbitrary fashion.

DON'T miss this

Keeping records of complaints also allows HR to review for possible patterns of harassment, discrimination or other misconduct by the same individual.

Document facts, not conclusions

Good documentation is specific and objective. Don't use labels—they compromise the documentation's objectivity. Characterizations, adjectives and adverbs should be used sparingly, if at all. Avoid making broad, general statements or unsupported conclusions.

> ***Example:*** *Don't document that "Raj said Marissa was upset by Ken's rude behavior." You have made unsupported conclusions that Marissa was "upset" and that Ken's behavior was "rude." Instead, record that "Raj heard Ken tell Marissa in a loud voice, 'you don't belong in a man's job and should be home taking care of your husband and family,'" and that "within a few minutes of hearing this comment, Raj saw Marissa begin to cry and leave the room."*

Do *not* attempt to reach a legal conclusion in the documentation. Instead, deal with the facts, be specific and tell a story. The goal is to document what people have actually said or done.

> ***Example:*** *Don't say that William sexually harassed Margo. Sexual harassment is for a judge or jury to determine. Instead, say that William repeatedly asked Margo to date him over her stated objections, repeatedly made sexual comments to Margo, and repeatedly complained about his marital relations to Margo, again over her objections. Once you have specified the facts, you can then categorize it as inappropriate or unprofessional conduct according to your employer's policy.*

Take clear, detailed notes— leave your tape recorder at home

Take clear, detailed notes of interviews and other investigation activities. Notes should also be accurate, legible and free of spelling and grammatical errors so they cannot be used later to discredit the investigator. The date, time, place, and names of people present should appear at the top of the notes. These notes then can be used to write either a short, hand-written summary or a more extensive report on the situation.

It is not necessary to tape-record interviews. If your notes are well-taken, they will be sufficient. There may be some advantages to tape-recording interviews—it gives you an exact recording of what happened in the interview and allows you to focus on listening to the witness' answers, rather than on taking lots of notes. However, the disadvantages usually outweigh the advantages. The disadvantages of tape-recording interviews include:

- Causing the witness to become unnecessarily guarded—you want the witness to be at ease so that he/she will speak candidly with you;
- Tape-recording could be expensive, especially if you have the tapes transcribed;
- Technology/functionality problems—for example, it may turn out that the tape recorder does not record everything that was said during the interview because the tape malfunctioned, wasn't turned over at the right time, etc.; and
- Some states require that all parties to the conversation give permission before being taped.

Thus, when interviewing, avoid tape recorders. Stick with note-taking, and take the time during the interview to refer to your notes, to ask clarifying questions, and to review their accuracy with the interviewee. Reference to your notes will make you a more careful interviewer.

What if the witness makes a request to tape-record the interview?

You are not required to allow an employee to tape the interview. Indeed, honoring this type of request is usually a bad idea because the employee may distribute their tape recording to others, and consequently, lessen the privacy and integrity of the investigation. If you do allow the witness to tape the interview, you should tape it as well.

Get a "sign off" from each interview

Employees who are interviewed should be asked to sign the interview summary, sign an acknowledgement or write their own version of the event. Employees who do not want to sign a "statement" may be willing to sign an acknowledgement or may prefer to write a separate version of the event.

In addition, after each interview, have the employee "sign off" on the notes you have taken. Give them a chance to scribble in their own notations if they wish to comment on or add to your notes.

Final review

Before documentation is filed in an employee's personnel file, ask another manager or a human resources representative to read and sign off on it. This final review ensures that no improper comments are contained in the file. It also ensures consistency with organization policy and procedure and that there is an accurate record that can be relied upon to explain the action that results from the investigation.

The reviewer should be someone who is trained and familiar with both the laws under which an individual could bring a legal action as a result of disciplinary documentation and with your organization's policy. It also must be someone who has been authorized by your organization's lawyer to have access to this kind of documentation.

✓ Checklist

These are some of the things that you should look for when reviewing documentation of a disciplinary incident.

- ☐ Is it complete?
- ☐ Is it specific?
- ☐ Is it clear?
- ☐ Is it relevant?
- ☐ Does it avoid labels and conclusions (*i.e.* is it objective)?
- ☐ Is it factual and accurate?
- ☐ Is it consistent?
- ☐ Is it "fresh"—how much time elapsed between the incident and the write up?

Document retention

Records of employment actions taken as a result of an investigation should be retained in case the action is challenged by the employee as arbitrary or unreasonable in a grievance proceeding, during arbitration, or by filing a complaint with a government agency. Similarly, documentation can be useful evidence if an employer is called upon to defend its actions in a court of law. In addition, records should be maintained after the investigation concludes because they could be used to establish patterns and practices of behavior in the future.

How long should a record be kept?

Organizations usually have policies on the length of time documentation is retained and provide for removal and destruction after a certain period of time if there are no further disciplinary events. These time periods range from 12 months to five years. In some organizations, documentation may be retained indefinitely as a permanent part of the employee's file.

Federal law requires employers to retain records of some job-related events, although disciplinary records and performance evaluations are not specifically among them. Title VII of the Civil Rights Act of 1964, the Americans with Disabilities Act, and the Age Discrimination in Employment Act all require that records of demotions, transfers and layoffs be kept for one year. Title VII and the ADA also require that records of involuntarily terminated employees must be kept for a period of one year from the date of termination. And, if a discrimination charge is brought, all relevant personnel records must be kept until the case is finally resolved.

Note that personnel records relevant to a discrimination charge must be retained until the charge or resulting litigation is completely resolved. It is wrong to knowingly or intentionally destroy records relevant to pending or ongoing litigation, even if your internal policies would otherwise permit you to do so. Following the Enron scandal, Congress passed the Sarbanes-Oxley Act to tighten laws governing corporate fraud and accountability. One part of that act criminalizes the destruction (or alteration) of any corporate records with the intent to interfere or influence a government investigation, either relating to or "in contemplation of" an official government proceeding. As a practical matter, this means that it would be wise to consult with legal counsel before destroying any employment records that potentially might result in litigation, even if no charge or lawsuit has been filed.

Some state laws require that personnel files must be retained for a given period of time following an employee's termination. These retention periods range from 60 days to three years following termination; check your own states' laws for details.

Retention requirements for federal contractors. For employers that are federal contractors, record retention requirements vary depending on whether the contractor employs 150 or more employees and whether the contractor has a federal contract of at least $150,000. For contractors with fewer than 150 employees or who do not have a federal contract of at least $150,000, the minimum record retention period is one year from the date the record is made or the personnel action involved occurs, whichever occurs later. In addition, when an employee is involuntarily terminated, keep the personnel records of that employee for a period of one year from the date of the termination.

For contractors with 150 or more employees or who have a federal contract of at least $150,000, the minimum record retention period is two years from the date the record is made or the personnel action involved occurs, whichever occurs later. In addition, when an employee is involuntarily terminated, keep the personnel records of that employee for a period of two years from the date of the termination. Again, if a discrimination charge is brought, all relevant personnel records must be kept until the case is finally resolved.

Documentation of the investigative process should not be placed in individual employee's personnel files, unless it is determined that inappropriate conduct occurred and that discipline is necessary. Remember that everything in a personnel file may be subject to a subpoena. If there are documents you wish to keep absolutely confidential, you may be able to do so by giving them to your attorney so they are protected by the attorney-client privilege. Remember, however, that you may still have to testify as to what you know is contained in these documents.

> Preserve the complete record in a safe, confidential manner for at least as long as may be required by any applicable regulatory or state statute of limitations. Access to these documents should only be allowed on a "need to know" basis. Those with a need to know may include: the company lawyers, CEO, HR director, and any outside investigators. Generally, the fewer individuals who have access to disciplinary documentation, the better.

Medical records

Sometimes when exploring the reasons underlying employment problems, the ensuing investigations reveal employee medical conditions. When that happens, the discussions with employees may evolve from an investigative nature to that of an interactive process for accommodating a worker with a disability.

Documentation of the accommodation process, while valuable to the defense of a charge of failure to accommodate, is no longer part of the "disciplinary" documentation and becomes subject to special rules under the Americans with Disabilities Act relating to the confidentiality of medical records. This type of documentation must be maintained in separate, confidential medical files.

Polygraph records

In most instances, the Employee Polygraph Protection Act prohibits private employers from requiring employees to take a lie detector test. Under limited circumstances, however, an employer can still require an employee to submit to a polygraph. If an employee is already under suspicion on the basis of independent evidence, the employee may be asked to take a polygraph as part of an ongoing investigation of economic loss or injury, such as theft or embezzlement, to the employer's business.

Public employers are not subject to the law. Thus, government employers at the federal, state and local level can test employees outside of the context of an ongoing investigation.

Employers who are permitted to require polygraph testing must follow special rules about documenting the testing. The Employee Polygraph Protection Act requires employers to retain certain documentation for three years from the date a polygraph exam is conducted or requested, including:

- A copy of the statement that sets forth the specific incident or activity under investigation and the basis for testing a particular employee.
- Records specifically identifying the loss or injury in question and the nature of the employee's access to the person or property that is the subject of the investigation.
- All opinion lists and other records relating to polygraph tests of such persons and any charges stemming from them.

The Quiz

1. Good documentation does not include:
   a. Conclusions
   b. Objective recitation of the facts
   c. Employee involvement
   d. Review by someone other than the originator

2. An employee, Walt, did not report for work on Friday because his car wouldn't start. On Monday, his supervisor asked for a receipt showing that he had the car repaired, but the employee did not have one. Which documentation of the incident is the best one, "a" or "b"?
   a. "Walt lied."
   b. "On Monday, March 6, 2000, Walt said he couldn't come to work last Friday because his car broke down. I asked him for receipts for repairs. He couldn't provide them. I asked him the names of the garage where the repairs were done and he couldn't remember."

3. Inconsistent documentation can be used to show that someone was investigated/disciplined for discriminatory reasons. ❑ True ❑ False

4. In most cases, the minimum retention period for records relating to an investigation should be:
   a. Six months
   b. One year
   c. Five years
   d. Indefinitely

5. The timeliness of documentation is not important. ❑ True ❑ False

Answer key: 1. a; 2. b; 3. T; 4. b; 5. F.

Chapter 7

Reach a conclusion and write your investigative report

Reach a conclusion	110
BEST PRACTICES: Solutions to remedy the unsolvable complaint	114
No job is complete until the paperwork is done!	115
Get approval from your legal advisor	117
Who should see the report?	117
Keep track of all copies of the final report drafts	118
Who should know about the results?	118
The Quiz	120

You have completed your investigation of an incident involving two co-workers, Felix and Isabella. Isabella claims that Felix made rude, offensive comments to her. Felix claims that Isabella slapped him across the face without any provocation on his part. You must now come to a conclusion about what happened and provide a written report to management on the conclusion(s) reached as a result of your investigation.

Reach a conclusion

Once the investigation is completed, the next step is to make a determination as to whether a violation of the employer's policies or other misconduct has occurred. By the time the investigation has ended, your conclusion(s) may be fairly obvious. However, before you reach a conclusion, you should review the documentation, determine the credibility of the witnesses, and weigh the facts.

Attempting to resolve a complaint to the satisfaction of all concerned (to the extent possible and reasonable) should be HR's main objective. Whatever the result, it is important to ensure that any determination is well-founded and solidly supported by facts in the investigative record.

Analyze the data—base your conclusion on the facts and records

Review the documentation. As you review your documentation:
- Make sure your documentation is complete;
- Determine if there are any conflicting statements; and
- Remove anything that is not relevant (that is, anything that does not tend to prove or disprove the allegation being investigated).

By sticking to the goals you established at the beginning of the investigation, and by concentrating on gathering only relevant evidence during the investigation, you should end up with documentation that proves, or disproves the underlying allegation(s).

For detailed discussion of what documentation you should have, see Chapter 6.

Determine the credibility of witnesses. Consider the following factors when making credibility determinations:
- Inherent plausibility of the person's story;
- Demeanor of parties and witnesses;
- Motivation to lie;
- Corroboration of allegations; and
- Past records of the employee making the complaint and the accused.

You may wish to consider other factors if they are relevant.

"He said, she said" situations. When investigating claims such as workplace harassment, the resolution often depends upon the credibility of the parties because such harassment often happens in private with no witnesses. Unfortunately, these "he said, she said" situations may be the rule and not the exception. How do you handle a situation where it comes down to weighing two different stories of what happened?

The Equal Employment Opportunity Commission (EEOC) and juries can find that workplace harassment occurred based solely on the victim's description of what happened. This means that the fact that there are no other witnesses does not *automatically* mean that the employer should take no action against the accused.

Consider the following in evaluating a "he said, she said" situation. In order to find that the victim is believable, the EEOC gives great weight to a victim's ability to provide a sufficiently detailed and internally consistent account of the events. If the employee is unable to present any facts that support his or her story, the complaint will be perceived as less believable.

✓ Checklist
Factors to help determine whether harassment occurred

A general denial by the accused will carry little weight with the EEOC when other supporting evidence exists. HR should look for surrounding evidence to support or disprove a harassment claim. Such evidence may be found by asking the following questions:

☐ Do coworkers have any knowledge of the conduct?
☐ Did anyone observe the victim's behavior shortly after the alleged incident of harassment? The accused's behavior?
☐ Did the victim discuss the matter with another person such as a counselor, doctor or close friend?
☐ Did anyone notice any change in the victim's behavior at work or in the way that the alleged harasser treated the victim?
☐ Were other employees treated in a similar manner by the alleged harasser?

Weigh the facts. What standard of proof should you use to arrive at your decision? Use a more likely than not standard (what lawyers would call a "preponderance of the evidence standard"). This is the standard used in most civil lawsuits and is usually the most appropriate standard to use when making a determination regarding an internal investigation.

Remember that while the goal is to have an outcome that is favorable to the company, your job is to make a fair and complete investigation of what occurred.

If you bypass unfavorable evidence, testimony or documentation, be certain that, in the event that a lawsuit, government agency complaint, or union grievance is filed, the opposition will not.

Arrive at a fair, objective and defensible conclusion

Again, whatever conclusion you reach, it is important to ensure that it is fair, well-founded and solidly supported by facts in the investigative record. Generally, you will come to one of two possible conclusions:

(1) The allegations have been proved, and you can recommend (or implement, if you have such authority) a course of action (see Chapter 8);

(2) The allegation has not been proved—the results of the investigation reveal that there is no substance to the allegation; no disciplinary action is warranted, unless you determine someone has made a false complaint, in which case you should consider imposing discipline (see Chapter 8).

You may not have the authority to implement discipline, but as the investigator (or part of the investigation team) you may be called upon to recommend an appropriate course of action. If you've investigated the matter in good faith and concluded that a particular course of action is recommended, it shouldn't be difficult to convince management of your decision. However, you should anticipate possible objections to your recommendation (and how you will answer them) before you present it to management. You should have an answer ready for each objection.

If you are prepared to recommend and/or implement discipline, be sure that the action you recommend is proportional to the seriousness of the offense. See Chapter 8 for a discussion regarding implementing discipline.

The hard-to-resolve claim

Some claims, such as workplace harassment, are especially difficult. HR may do everything right, but conflicting evidence may make it impossible to determine whether workplace harassment has occurred. This happens most often in what is sometimes referred to as the "he said, she said" situation. The victim of the claimed harassment might make a complaint like this about a coworker: "He made off-color jokes I was supposed to laugh at, stared provocatively at me, and brushed himself against me on several occasions."

When HR questions the accused harasser, however, he may declare with great certainty and apparent honesty, "Yes, I made off-color jokes, but I was careful. I watched to see how she was taking them, and she always seemed to smile. But that's all I did; I never 'stared' at her, and I certainly didn't 'brush myself against her.'"

What is HR looking at in a case like this? If both employees stick to their stories—"He's harassed me" and "No, I haven't"—and there are no witnesses, HR may never know what actually occurred.

Bring closure. Even in these difficult situations, it is important for HR to bring closure. HR does know that a complaint of harassment has been made. Even if you can't determine what actually happened, it is important that the complaint be resolved. HR should bring the complaint to some formal conclusion through investigation and communication with all parties involved. The steps in the process and the final resolution should be documented. For a discussion of documentation, see Chapter 6.

At the very least, HR should:
- ◆ Reemphasize to all parties involved in the complaint the employer's prohibition of harassment and discrimination in the workplace.
- ◆ Document that a complaint was received and an investigation took place, but that it could not be determined if inappropriate conduct actually occurred.

- Reassure the complaining employee that he or she will be protected from retaliation (that is, his or her employment conditions will not be adversely affected by the complaint) and urge him or her to immediately report any future incidents of workplace harassment.
- Advise the accused employee that everyone is expected to comply with the organization's policies.

If the complaint can't be proven either way, do not discipline either the alleged harasser or the victim.

Of course, there is no guarantee that the victim will not take the complaint elsewhere—such as to a lawyer or even to the EEOC, state agency or union grievance authority. But taking steps to resolve the complaint will put HR in a much better position to explain the organization's position should the need ever arise.

Best Practices

Solutions to remedy the unsolvable complaint

Legal experts at Jackson Lewis, a national employment law firm representing management, suggest that where the results of an investigation do not clearly suggest whether harassment has occurred, HR's best ally in fashioning a response may be the complaining employee. Continued communication with that employee regarding the outcome of the investigation and the action he or she would like taken in order to continue working comfortably often helps bring an otherwise inconclusive investigation to a close. Jackson Lewis suggests the following actions:

- Notify the complaining employee that after an investigation, his or her claims could not be substantiated.
- Thank the employee for coming forward and provide assurances of the employer's commitment to providing a work environment free of harassment.
- Tell the employee that the accused has been reminded of the employer's intolerance of any type of harassment.

- Encourage the employee to immediately report any further incidents of harassment. Reassure the accused that because the investigation proved inconclusive, he or she will suffer no punishment.
- Warn the accused that any subsequent allegations might result in more severe discipline.
- Remind the accused of the employer's anti-harassment policy and the penalties for violating it.

If the complaining employee is not satisfied with this response, other options may be available. For example, is it possible to transfer one of the workers or to alter work schedules so they no longer work together? If possible, these options should be made available so that it is clear that HR is doing all that it can to resolve the situation to everyone's satisfaction. If separating the two is not possible, providing the entire department with additional training may be an appropriate solution.

If you decide to separate the victim and harasser, be careful! Any transfer must not appear to disadvantage the person making the harassment complaint. If the person making the complaint is reassigned, for example, to a less desirable position or to a position with few promotion opportunities, the employer may be seen as retaliating against the person for making a complaint.

No job is complete until the paperwork is done!

Finalize the investigation by preparing a preliminary investigative report, and obtain the approval of your legal counsel. Writing a report forces the investigator to think through the investigation's findings carefully. A written report is a document that decision-makers can use in determining the appropriate action. Moreover, a complete and accurate report is necessary to show that an employer promptly and thoroughly investigated a complaint and that its resolution of the complaint was appropriate.

WHAT you need to know

The report, as with all other documentation of the investigation, can be invaluable in defending against a wrongful discharge or defamation lawsuit by a person found guilty of misconduct. Therefore, the report must hold up under scrutiny by courts and juries. That means you need to know what they will be looking for in final documentation.

Model report format

Suggested components of the report include:
- The date the investigation was started and the date it was concluded;
- Statement of complaint (if applicable) or reason for investigation;
- Basis in policy or law;
- Names of witnesses interviewed;
- Witness summaries;
- List of documents;
- Statement of factual findings; and
- Statement of conclusions reached.

A recommended action, if you have the responsibility for doing so, should be put into a separate document. See Chapter 8 for a discussion of appropriate disciplinary action.

Statement of factual findings. When writing your summary of the facts, describe the relevant fact in narrative form. Don't just give a summary of what was said in each interview; instead, write a chronological narrative of what occurred. Be sure to include all sides of the story. Give sources for each factual statement you make. One way is to indicate in the narrative the source of the statement. For example, "[A]ccording to Felix, Isabella slapped him across the face." Another way is to include footnotes listing the source of each factual statement, especially if your factual narrative is lengthy. For example, "Isabella slapped Felix across the face.[1]" (with footnote 1 citing to "Interview with Felix, May 1, 2003.")

Avoid liability for defamation by sticking to the facts. Do not include your conclusions, recommendations, or personal opinions in your statement of factual findings.

Statement of conclusion(s) reached. Describe your credibility determinations and give factual support for each of the conclusions you reached. As a general rule, state your conclusions as factual findings, not legal conclusions. For example, don't write, "I conclude that Wanda created a hostile working environment for Todd based on Todd's disability." Instead write, "I conclude that Wanda repeatedly made jokes about Todd's alcohol addiction after Todd told her that he did not welcome such jokes."

Summary. Include a brief summary of your findings.

Appendices. Include a copy of any written statements provided by the complainant or the accused. Include other important documents that you refer to in your report. You do not need to include your interview notes.

Get approval from your legal advisor

Be aware that the report is "discoverable" in litigation. This means that if the person who made the complaint or the accused later sues, he or she will almost certainly see a copy of the report. Do *not* include any discussions with your attorney in the report. When the report is finalized, all previous drafts should be destroyed—they could be used against you in court.

Who should see the report?

Generally, only those involved in the decision-making process should see the report. Clarify with your attorney who in the organization can have access to the documents or information. Give or show the final report only to those people who must see them in order to take personnel actions.

Although you should generally advise the complaining employee of your conclusion (see below), you should not give the report to that employee.

If you use an internal investigator (that is, an investigator employed by your organization), you should not give the report to the accused. However, if you use an outside investigator who regularly conducts third party investigations, you will probably need to follow the procedures required under the Fair Credit Reporting Act. This means that you must provide a copy of the report, and all other investigative materials, to the accused before taking any disciplinary or other adverse action. In addition, you must give the target of the investigation the opportunity to dispute any inaccuracies that they perceive are in the report before taking any disciplinary or other adverse action. Be sure to clarify with your attorney what your obligations to the accused are under the Fair Credit Reporting Act.

According to the Federal Trade Commission, employers that hire outside organizations to investigate misconduct claims must follow Fair Credit Reporting Act (FCRA) procedures. The FTC believes that an outside investigator conducting an investigation on behalf of an employer is a "consumer reporting agency." Therefore, the report would most likely be an "investigative consumer report." Violations requiring disciplinary action could reasonably be defined as an adverse employment decision. Therefore, if HR plans on hiring an outside party to conduct the investigation, be sure to follow the FCRA rules. If unsure, consult with legal counsel for guidance.

Keep track of all copies of the final report drafts

Copies of the final report may be shown to those who have a "need to know," but make sure that each and every copy is returned to the investigator for destruction. Generally, the fewer individuals who have access to disciplinary documentation, the better.

Who should know about the results?

What should you tell the person who made the complaint?

Inform the person who made the complaint of the conclusion(s) you reached and why you reached that conclusion. You should always tell the complaining employee whether you found his or her allegations credible. However, you should only advise the person who made the complaint of the outcome *after* you have completed your report and discussed it, and any possible actions that may be warranted, with management.

Chapter 7—Reach a conclusion and write your investigative report

You should inform the person who made the complaint of any course of action that will affect him or her. For instance, if you have ordered an accused harasser to stay away from the person who complained, you should inform the victim of this order. If there is no applicable law or employment agreement barring you from disclosing the punishment received by the accused, you can probably tell the person who made the complaint about the punishment also, but you should check with your legal counsel before doing so. For a detailed discussion on what to tell the person making the complaint about disciplinary action taken, see Chapter 8.

In addition, you should encourage the employee who has complained to report future incidents that he or she believes constitute harassment, retaliation or other misconduct, and ask the complaining employee to keep the matter confidential.

What should you tell the target of the investigation?

Inform the accused of:
- The conclusion(s) you reached;
- Why you reached the conclusion;
- The disciplinary action, if any (see Chapter 8 for a detailed discussion); and
- the organization's policy against retaliation.

The target of the investigation will likely have the following questions:
- Who was involved in the decision-making process?;
- Can the conclusion be appealed?;
- Who will know about the disciplinary action?; and
- How will the discipline affect his or her future in the organization?

For a discussion of implementing discipline, see Chapter 8.

Do I have to tell the other witnesses anything?

There is no need to consult with witnesses after the investigation is completed. If witnesses ask about the results of your investigation, inform them that the results are confidential, and thank them for their cooperation in the investigation.

The Quiz

1. A written report of an investigation should not include which of the following:
   a. A statement of factual findings.
   b. A recommendation as to a course of disciplinary action.
   c. A statement of the conclusion(s) reached.
   d. An appendix of relevant documents.

2. When weighing the facts, the standard of proof you should use is:
   a. Beyond any doubt.
   b. Beyond a reasonable doubt.
   c. More likely than not.

3. After investigating a situation in which it is impossible to determine whether harassment or other misconduct has occurred, HR should simply give up and do nothing. ❑ True ❑ False

4. If witnesses, other than the person who made the complaint or the target of the investigation, ask about the results of your investigation, you should tell them that the results are confidential. ❑ True ❑ False

Answer key: 1. b; 2. c; 3. F; 4. T

Chapter 8

Now that the investigation is over ...

Good faith is the guiding principle	122
Arrive at a fair, objective and defensible decision	122
Any disciplinary action must "fit the crime"	123
BEST PRACTICES: Be prepared before disciplining	124
BEST PRACTICES: Postal Service picks suitable discipline for questionable conduct	126
BEST PRACTICES: Quick corrective action excuses liability at trial	130
Preventing retaliation	131
Follow applicable procedures	132
Addressing the accused, the victim and the workforce	133
Following up	137
Don't forget to document the process!	138
The Quiz	139

Ravi, a Hindi employee, has made a complaint to the HR office, stating that he has been the victim of ethnic harassment. You have investigated the complaint by reviewing relevant documents. You have also interviewed Ravi and the two coworkers he accused of harassment, Colin and Joe. In addition, you have interviewed their supervisor, Renee, and the other coworker in the group, Juanita. In short, the interviews went as follows.

Ravi was believable and gave a detailed description of his side of the story. He accused Colin and Joe of making off-color jokes about his ethnic background. He reported feeling isolated from his group and unable to perform as well as his coworkers.

Colin and Joe denied acting in a harassing or discriminatory manner. They both admitted that they had made ethnic

> jokes, but claimed that Ravi participated by making jokes about their ethnic backgrounds—Irish and Italian. They claimed that it was all in good fun and that they had no idea that Ravi was offended. Renee had no knowledge of inappropriate comments by Colin or Joe—to Ravi or anyone else in the workplace. She has noticed that Ravi has been "keeping to himself" and has been taking a lot of time off lately.
>
> Juanita recalled several times when Colin and Joe "teased" Ravi about not being a "true American." She also remembered one time when she heard Colin call Ravi a "smelly camel rider." That time Ravi walked away and didn't return to the work area for several minutes. Juanita didn't recall Ravi ever commenting about Colin's or Joe's ethnicity.
>
> You have come to the conclusion that Colin and Joe engaged in inappropriate conduct and have written a report regarding you investigation and conclusion. Now, you must recommend a course of action to management. How do you determine what course of action to recommend?

Good faith is the guiding principle

After you have reached your conclusion and written your investigative report (see Chapter 7), you must decide or recommend, depending upon your duties and authority, if discipline is warranted and what the appropriate discipline, if any, should be.

Remember that all investigations must be conducted in good faith (in other words, without any preconceived intention to "get" a particular individual). Even if you mistakenly discipline an innocent person, you should be able to avoid legal liability if you conducted the investigation in good faith, arrived at a reasonable conclusion, and implemented appropriate discipline if warranted.

Arrive at a fair, objective and defensible decision

Once you have determined whether a violation of the employer's policies or other misconduct has occurred, you (or someone with the appropriate authority) must decide what action will be taken based on the findings.

Convincing management to follow your recommendation should not be difficult if you've investigated the matter in good faith. However, you should anticipate possible objections to your recommendation before you present it to management. Have an answer ready for each objection. Your recommendation may not be implemented, but that will not be due to any act or omission on your part.

Companies responding to a 1999 survey by the Society for Human Resource Management (SHRM) revealed that, after investigation, two out of three (65 percent) sexual harassment complaints were substantiated. Those complaints that were substantiated resulted in a warning (29 percent) or some form of disciplinary action against the alleged harassers.

See Chapter 7 for a discussion on what actions to take for a "hard-to-resolve" claim.

Any disciplinary action must "fit the crime"

Choose the proper discipline

If HR concludes that harassment or other misconduct has occurred, HR must decide how to appropriately discipline the offending supervisor or employee who was responsible for the misconduct. If you are prepared to recommend and/or implement discipline, be sure that the action is in proportion to the seriousness of the offense. Consider the following factors:
- Severity, pervasiveness and frequency of the conduct;
- Position of the harasser within the organization;
- Previous discipline received; and
- Your employment policies, such as progressive discipline.

Best Practices

Be prepared before disciplining

Whatever the reason for disciplinary action, the best solution is to be prepared. Lynn Outwater, J.D., a partner with the law firm of Jackson, Lewis, Schnitzler & Krupman, developed this checklist:

- Know all the facts accurately.
- Review how other employees were disciplined—is this employee receiving the same treatment others have received for the same offense?
- Is the rule that has been violated reasonable?
- Did the employee know the rule—or should he or she have known the rule?
- Is the rule being applied reasonably?
- Have any preliminary procedures been followed?
- Except in cases such as observed theft, assault and other dangerous or harmful offenses, has the employee first been warned?
- Is this employee personally guilty, rather than being guilty by association with another?
- Does the discipline fit the misconduct?
- What is the employee's disciplinary record?
- How long has the employee been with your organization?
- Does the employee have a reasonable excuse for the rule infraction or misconduct?
- Can the employee's responsibility for the rule infraction or misconduct be proven by direct, objective evidence or only by circumstantial evidence or conjecture?
- Did you have an opportunity to deter this employee from committing an offense and fail to do so?

Options for corrective action

Appropriate forms of discipline can include oral or written warnings, reprimands, demotion, suspension and probation. If the conduct is very offensive or if the offender's ability to perform his or her job is impaired significantly, discharge may be the only alternative. Lesser discipline should be accompanied by a warning that any similar misconduct in the future will result in immediate discharge. Depending on the circumstances, it may be enough to counsel the person who engaged in the misconduct and arrange for an apology. Or, if the conduct was more severe, HR may need to arrange for a transfer or reassignment (see below).

Options for corrective action include:
- No action;
- An apology made to the victim, if there was one;
- Corrective training for an individual or the whole workforce;
- Oral reprimand;
- Written reprimand;
- Probation;
- Suspension;
- Demotion;
- Separate the parties—but don't transfer or otherwise burden the victim without his or her written permission;
- Reduction in salary; and
- Dismissal.

Make sure that your organization's harassment policy allows you to discipline employees for harassing behavior even if the behavior is not so severe or pervasive that it meets the legal definition of unlawful harassment. For example, consider Ravi's situation. It appears that Colin and Joe did make derogatory statements to Ravi about his ethnic heritage. While the behavior may or may not violate federal law, it is inappropriate and must be stopped. Colin and Joe should be disciplined and monitored to make sure the behavior does not continue.

Can an oral warning suffice?

An oral warning may be the proper response where the conduct complained of is minor and isolated (such as a small number of "off color" remarks by an employee who has no prior history of similar misconduct). You should warn that further inappropriate conduct will result in more severe discipline.

As always, documentation is essential. Make a record of having administered the oral warning and provide the record to the person designated to handle harassment and discrimination complaints or other employee misconduct. Such records may later show a pattern of misconduct.

If the misconduct recurs, impose more severe discipline.

Best Practices
Postal Service picks suitable discipline for questionable conduct

The US Postal Service avoided liability for sexual harassment because it took appropriate corrective action by disciplining a male coworker found to have sexually harassed a female employee. The Postal Service learned of the alleged harasser's questionable conduct when another employee reported having seen the accused grab the female employee's hand with the intention of kissing it and refuse to let go despite her protests.

Management investigated within three days of the report. The accused's supervisor issued a reprimand for his conduct and warned him on two occasions to stay away from the female employee. Because the employee found the male employee's presence discomforting, management also moved her to a different job farther away from his area.

Although the victim argued in court that the Postal Service should have disciplined the male employee more extensively, the court disagreed. It viewed the admonishments as adequate discipline given that there were 16 reported incidents of harassing behavior, yet none of which were severe and per-

> vasive enough to create a hostile working environment. The discipline imposed, along with removing the female employee from the work area, stopped the harassment altogether and therefore was sufficient.

Transfers and reassignments

Be careful when separating victim and harasser. In some harassment cases it may be appropriate for HR to separate the victim and the harasser. Exercise extreme caution in this area.

Any transfer must not appear to disadvantage the person making the harassment complaint.

If the person making the complaint is reassigned, for example, to a less desirable position or to a position with few promotion opportunities, the employer may be seen as retaliating against the person for making a complaint.

- When attempting to remedy harassment, avoid requiring that the complaining employee work less desirable hours or in a less desirable location.
- If HR offers to transfer the complaining employee, try to get his or her consent and make sure the transfer position is substantially similar to his or her prior position. This helps ensure that the employee is not being illegally punished for opposing discrimination or harassment.

Be consistent

HR must make sure that all actions taken for violation of policy or other misconduct are not only timely, but also consistent with past practice. Sometimes employees who have been disciplined or terminated for misconduct will later claim that they were unlawfully discriminated against because of their sex, race, age or other protected characteristic. In other words, they say that they were treated differently from other employees accused of misconduct.

Therefore, before disciplining or discharging an employee accused of misconduct, you should carefully consider how the organization has treated other workers accused of similar behavior. To assist with this review, HR should maintain confidential records regarding disciplinary investigations and claims.

> If HR decides to change past procedures, be careful to evaluate any ramifications and consider how you will handle any behavior that occurred before the change was officially made. Remember, it is important that any disciplinary action be taken without regard to sex, age, race or any other protected status.

Take prompt action

HR must take prompt action when inappropriate workplace conduct is found. This means immediately doing whatever is necessary to stop the behavior. After all, the victim complained in hopes that the behavior would stop.

In "victimless" situations—where misconduct was not directly against any specific individual—HR must still take prompt action, or the organization runs the risk of tolerating behavior that is against stated policy. If stated policy isn't promptly and consistently enforced, the organization becomes more vulnerable to charges of discrimination because of inconsistent treatment.

Why is it so important that the action be prompt? In harassment situations, any delay in stopping known harassment sharply increases an employer's risk of liability should the victim decide to sue. Therefore, you must immediately take corrective action that is "reasonably calculated to stop the harassment and deter future harassment."

> *By acting promptly, HR sends a clear message to the workforce that inappropriate conduct and other violations of policy will not be tolerated.*

Chapter 8—Now that the investigation is over... **129**

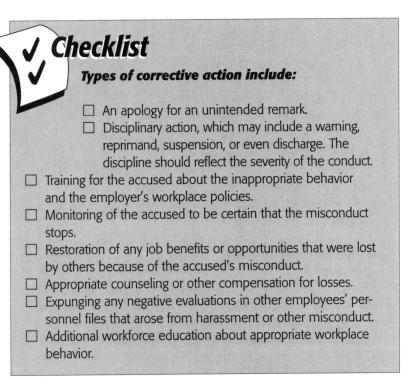

✓ Checklist
Types of corrective action include:

- ☐ An apology for an unintended remark.
- ☐ Disciplinary action, which may include a warning, reprimand, suspension, or even discharge. The discipline should reflect the severity of the conduct.
- ☐ Training for the accused about the inappropriate behavior and the employer's workplace policies.
- ☐ Monitoring of the accused to be certain that the misconduct stops.
- ☐ Restoration of any job benefits or opportunities that were lost by others because of the accused's misconduct.
- ☐ Appropriate counseling or other compensation for losses.
- ☐ Expunging any negative evaluations in other employees' personnel files that arose from harassment or other misconduct.
- ☐ Additional workforce education about appropriate workplace behavior.

The actions taken should be designed to correct the behavior and to prevent it from happening again. If there was a victim of the misconduct, your overall goal should be to place the employee who complained in the position that he or she would have been in if the misconduct had not occurred in the first place.

WHAT you need to know

If an employee files an EEOC charge, what does the EEOC look for in terms of actions by the employer? The EEOC looks to see if the employer did several key things, said EEOC senior trial attorney June Wallace Carson during the 2000 Technical Assistance Program Seminar in Lincolnshire, Illinois:
- ◆ What, if anything, did the employer do in response to the employee's complaint?
- ◆ Was the action taken appropriate to the circumstances?
- ◆ Was the action taken effective?
- ◆ Was the misconduct eliminated and was the victim made whole?

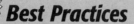

Best Practices

Quick corrective action excuses liability at trial

A court ruled that an employer's immediate and appropriate corrective action excused the employer from sexual harassment liability under federal law. In this case, an employee complained to her employer that her coworker had talked to her about sexual activities and touched her in an offensive manner. Within four days of receiving the complaint, the employer did the following:

- investigated the charges;
- reprimanded the guilty employee;
- placed him on probation; and
- warned him that further misconduct would result in discharge.

A second coworker who had witnessed the harassment was also reprimanded for not intervening on the victim's behalf or reporting the misconduct.

The false complaint

What if an allegation of misconduct turns out to be false?

You should discipline an employee who files a false complaint, but *only* if you find conclusive evidence that the employee who made the complaint *intentionally* made a false complaint.

It is important for HR to determine whether the person who made the complaint deliberately lied or simply misunderstood the conduct alleged. Don't impose discipline on the complaining party unless you are absolutely certain that the person was fully aware that the claim was false at the time he or she made it. Discipline of someone who mistakenly reported perceived misconduct not only can discourage employees from making complaints, but can also result in being sued for retaliation.

How severely can you discipline someone who files a false complaint? Generally, you should punish an employee who makes a false complaint in the same way that you would punish an employee who makes an untruthful statement of similar seriousness. In other words, if discipline is warranted, it should be consistent with that imposed for dishonesty in comparable circumstances.

Do not discipline the employee making the complaint simply because there was insufficient evidence to support the employee's allegations, or simply because the conduct occurred but did not violate a law or employment policy.

Preventing retaliation

Failure to stop negative actions against an employee who complains of misconduct or someone who participates in a workplace investigation can result in liability for an employer, regardless of the outcome of the investigation. Federal law prohibits such retaliation, as does the law in most states.

An employer can be held legally responsible not only for retaliatory actions by managers and supervisors but also for those by coworkers. Just as an employer must promptly and effectively stop harassment, it must do the same with respect to retaliatory activity.

What is retaliation?

Some of the most obvious types of unlawful retaliation are denying a promotion, denying job benefits, demotion, suspension and discharge. Retaliation may also take the form of threats, reprimands, negative evaluations, and harassment.

Unlawful retaliation can occur even after the employment relationship ends. For example, a negative job reference may be viewed by a court as retaliatory if the reason the bad reference was provided was to "punish" the worker for having participated in an investigation.

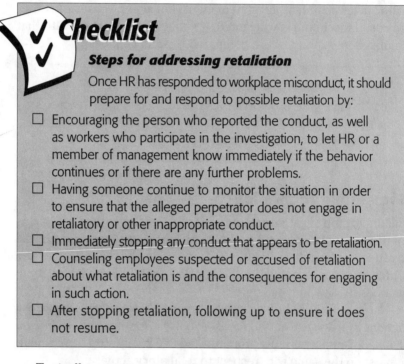

✓ Checklist

Steps for addressing retaliation

Once HR has responded to workplace misconduct, it should prepare for and respond to possible retaliation by:

☐ Encouraging the person who reported the conduct, as well as workers who participate in the investigation, to let HR or a member of management know immediately if the behavior continues or if there are any further problems.
☐ Having someone continue to monitor the situation in order to ensure that the alleged perpetrator does not engage in retaliatory or other inappropriate conduct.
☐ Immediately stopping any conduct that appears to be retaliation.
☐ Counseling employees suspected or accused of retaliation about what retaliation is and the consequences for engaging in such action.
☐ After stopping retaliation, following up to ensure it does not resume.

Typically, very severe penalties, including discharge, are applied to individuals who retaliate, especially after having been warned not to do so in the course of an investigation. After a warning, additional corrective actions should be considered, such as meetings, statements and training focusing on the employer's strict prohibition of retaliation and what constitutes retaliation.

Be ready to back up your anti-retaliation policy with suitable discipline if and when a violation occurs.

Follow applicable procedures

In addition to conducting your investigation in good faith, being consistent when implementing discipline, taking prompt action, and guarding against retaliation, you should follow your organization's disciplinary procedures. This will help your organization avoid any due process, breach of contract, wrongful discharge, and/or discrimination lawsuits.

> What are the elements of workplace due process?
> - **General notice.** The employee knows the employer's expectations.
> - **Specific notice.** The employee receives notice of any failure to meet the employer's expectations and understands the consequences.
> - **Administration.** Rules and regulations are administered consistently.
> - **Appeals.** There is a viable internal appeals procedure.

WHAT you need to know

If you are a government employer, the accused could bring a lawsuit alleging denial of "due process" and other claims if you don't follow the civil service rules. Union employees may bring suit if the disciplinary procedures set forth in your collective bargaining agreement are not followed. If the employee has an employment contract, follow any disciplinary procedures set forth in that contract.

Addressing the accused, the victim and the workforce

What should you tell the target of the investigation?

As discussed in Chapter 7, you should inform the target of the investigation of the conclusion(s) you reached and why you reached them. To be fair and avoid a potential lawsuit, you should give the accused details of the allegations and witness statements (including identifying the witnesses), and a chance to respond before you take any disciplinary action. In addition, you should remind the accused of your organization's policy against retaliation.

If you decide to implement disciplinary action against the accused, you should, of course, inform him or her what that action will be.

You may also want to discuss with the accused what the consequences of any further misconduct could be. If your company has a progressive disciplinary policy (or if one is provided for in a collective bargaining or other employment agreement), you may wish to review the policy with the accused.

Be prepared to answer questions from the accused, such as:
- Who was involved in the decision-making process;
- Can the decision be appealed;
- Who will know about the disciplinary action; and
- How will the discipline affect his or her future in the organization?

*If you use an outside investigator who regularly conducts third party investigations, be aware of the procedures required under the Fair Credit Reporting Act (FCRA). According to the Federal Trade Commission, employers that hire outside organizations to investigate misconduct claims must follow FCRA procedures. This means that you must provide a copy of the report, and all other investigative materials, to the accused **before** taking any disciplinary or other adverse action. In addition, you must give the target of the investigation the opportunity to dispute any inaccuracies that they perceive are in the investigative report before taking any disciplinary or other adverse action. Be sure to clarify with your attorney what your obligations to the accused are under the Fair Credit Reporting Act.*

What should you tell the person who made the complaint?

How much should you tell the person who made the initial complaint about the disciplinary action taken? Usually the person who reported the conduct should not be told the particulars of any disciplinary action, other than that the employer has acted appropriately to ensure that the misconduct will stop and will not reoccur. If you terminate someone based on an investigation, simply limit the explanation to, "[The employee] is no longer working here."

Although informing the employee who made the complaint about the details of the disciplinary action may help that employee assess whether the employer has taken the complaint seriously, that disclosure may leave the employer liable for a defamation or invasion or privacy suit from the accused. Be sure to check if your state or local laws, civil service rules, or collective bargaining agreements mandate that you keep disciplinary actions confidential.

Naturally, you should inform the person who made the complaint of any course of action that will affect him or her. For instance, if you have ordered an accused harasser to stay away from the person who complained, you should inform the victim of this order.

If you do decide to inform the person who made the complaint of the particulars of any disciplinary action taken, be sure to check with your legal counsel before doing so.

Sometimes, the person who made the complaint may feel badly because his or her complaint caused disciplinary action to be taken against the accused. In such cases, it may be helpful to remind the employee that the complaint helped prevent further misconduct from occurring. If the investigation turned up other information beyond the original complaint and, consequently, that complaint was not the only reason for the disciplinary action taken, explain that fact to the complaining employee.

What else should you tell the person who made the complaint? You should tell the person who made the complaint whether you found his or her allegations credible. It is important that the complaining employee understands that HR has taken or will take the appropriate steps to address the situation. In addition, you should remind him or her of your organization's policy against retaliation.

Addressing other needs of the victim. If warranted, HR should offer counseling services to the victim. This may be a good time to offer the company's Employee Assistance Program services, if available.

It may also be necessary to compensate the victim for any time he or she took away from work due to stress caused by the inappropriate behavior. HR must also address the victim's needs by restoring any job benefits or opportunities that may have been lost as a result of another's misconduct. This may include compensation for any lost pay or sick days used because of the stress related to the situation.

DON'T miss this

If someone with supervisory authority engaged in misconduct, or, in particular, harassed an employee, it is critical that HR check to ensure that no negative comments were made or negative job actions were taken for unlawful reasons. If they were, HR must take action to reverse the actions as quickly as possible.

✓ Checklist

Counseling the complaining employee

To help the employee accept HR's decision and get past the troubling situation, follow these steps:

☐ Give the employee making the complaint someone to talk to who will be sympathetic and credible to the employee.
☐ Help the employee understand what is and is not misconduct.
☐ Explain why HR has made the determination that it has and what it hopes to accomplish.
☐ Probe to be sure that the employee making the complaint feels secure about the immediate future.
☐ If the employee making a complaint fears harassment or other types of retaliation, explain what he or she should do about it given the situation.

What should you tell other employees?

Do you have to tell the witnesses to the investigation anything?

There is no need to consult with witnesses, other than the victim and the accused, after the investigation is completed. If witnesses ask about the results of your investigation, inform them that the results are confidential, and thank them for their cooperation in the investigation.

Keep in mind that disclosing the disciplinary action taken against the accused to other employees may leave the employer liable for a defamation or invasion of privacy suit from the accused. If you need to terminate someone based on an investigation, simply limit the explanation to, "[The employee] is no longer working here."

As with the accused and the person who made the complaint, you should remind the other witnesses of your organization's policy against retaliation.

Additional action may be necessary to prevent other misconduct. HR should use what was learned in the investigation as an opportunity to further reduce the risk of workplace misconduct. In addition to addressing the victim and the offender, HR may need to take additional corrective action designed to prevent potential misconduct. Consider Ravi's situation described at the beginning of this chapter—anti-harassment training is in order, at least for Colin and Joe; possibly for the entire workforce.

Sometimes an investigation will reveal that company policy is lacking in a certain area. Revising or amending the policy may be necessary.

Following up

Even if no additional complaints are made following an investigation, follow-up is necessary to make sure that the remedy has been effective to stop the misconduct and that no retaliation has been taken against any victim or witnesses.

Periodically follow up with the person who made the complaint to ensure that the misconduct has not recurred and that he or she is not suffering retaliation. Check with the accused's supervisor to make sure that there have been no additional problems.

If the remedy has been ineffective, it may be necessary to increase the level of discipline. HR's failure to follow up can result in liability if the misconduct continues.

Worst case scenario

After Joyce's first complaint of sexual harassment by a male coworker, management informed the coworker that his conduct must stop and warned him that discipline would result if the conduct resumed. But Joyce subsequently reported repeated instances of harassment by the coworker.

Management responded by adjusting the employees' shifts to reduce contact between them and by counseling the coworker and issuing additional oral warnings to him. Still, the harassment continued. The coworker was never reprimanded, issued a written warning, or disciplined in any manner.

Joyce took her claim to court and won. The court said that although management took corrective action, the employer was still liable because its actions were not reasonably designed to end the harassment.

Solution. HR must follow up to make sure that misconduct stops or the employer will face legal liability if the behavior continues. If a lesser degree of discipline has been ineffective, it may be necessary to take more severe measures to end workplace harassment.

Don't forget to document the process!

As detailed in Chapter 6, you should document any actions taken as a result of the investigation, as well as the reasons those actions were taken. If no action is taken, document the reasons why. In addition, be sure to document your action plan to follow-up on the actions taken as a result of the investigation.

The Quiz

1. If HR decides to transfer a victim of harassment in order to ensure that the behavior stops, it should:
   a. Avoid requiring that the victim work less desirable hours or in a less desirable location.
   b. Try to get the victim's consent.
   c. Make sure that the transfer position is substantially similar to the victim's prior position.
   d. All of the above.

2. To avoid legal liability when disciplining an employee, an employer should:
   a. Provide the accused details of the allegations and the identity of witnesses.
   b. Act in good faith.
   c. Be consistent.
   d. Follow applicable procedures.
   e. All of the above.

3. If HR investigates a complaint of misconduct and determines that inappropriate conduct did not occur, HR should:
   a. Immediately discipline the person who made the complaint.
   b. Determine whether the person deliberately lied or simply misperceived the misconduct alleged.
   c. Do nothing.

4. Once disciplinary action has been taken, there is no need for HR to follow-up unless another complaint is made.   ❑ True   ❑ False

Answer key: 1. d; 2. e; 3. b; 4. F.

Index

Assurance against reprisal ... 20

Best practices
   consumer credit report procedures ... 24
   corrective action excuses liability ... 130
   discipline, be prepared ... 124
   investigation plan preparation ... 36
   investigators, number of ... 57
   LEADER response ... 14
   model interview ... 88
   privacy expectation management ... 61
   remedying the unsolvable complaint ... 114
   response to reporting individual ... 17
   US Postal Service's response to questionable conduct ... 126

Checklists
   corrective action, types of ... 129
   counseling the complaining employee ... 136
   documentation review ... 103
   e-mail search, establishing employer's right to ... 67
   harassment determination ... 111
   interviewing dos and don'ts ... 74
   investigators
      characteristics, good ... 52
      outside, advantages of ... 54
      who not to select ... 49
   plan preparation ... 35
   records, relevant ... 42
   retaliation, responses to ... 132
   search implementation ... 64
   what to document ... 98
Closure ... 113
Communication
   checklists
      counseling the complaining employee ... 136

      to the accused ... 119, 133
      to the complaining employee ... 118, 134
      to witnesses ... 119, 136
Complaints
   anonymous ... 3
   best practices
      LEADER response ... 14
      response to reporting individual ... 17
   confidentiality ... 15
   delayed ... 10
   false ... 130
   government agency ... 4
   internal ... 2
   legal ... 5
   worst case scenarios
      delayed response ... 8
Conclusions ... 101, 110, 112, 117
   checklists
      harassment determination ... 111
Confidentiality ... 119
Consequences ... 43
Corrective action—*see also Discipline*
   best practices
      liability ... 130
   checklists
      types of ... 129
   generally ... 4, 125, 137
   worst case scenario
      continuing harassment ... 138
Credibility determinations
   best practices
      remedying the unsolvable complaint... 114
   factors ... 110
   he said, she said ... 111, 113

Defamation ... 21, 134, 136
Disability-related inquiries ... 26, 71

Discipline
  best practices
    be prepared ... *124*
    consistency ... *127*
    determinative factors ... *123*
    due process ... *133*
    good faith ... *122*
    records ... *128*
    oral warning ... *126*
    procedures ... *132*
Documentation
  checklists
    documentation review ... *103*
    relevant records ... *42*
    what to document ... *98*
  confidentiality ... *106*
  consistency ... *100*
  dating ... *96*
  destruction ... *104*
  discipline records ... *128*
  facts only ... *101*
  final review ... *103*
  generally ... *20, 138*
  importance of ... *96*
  medical records ... *106*
  notes—*see Notes*
  past documentation ... *97*
  polygraph records ... *106*
  relevant records ... *42*
  report—*see Report*
  retention
    federal contractors ... *105*
    generally ... *5*
    timeframes ... *104*
  timing ... *96*
  what to include ... *97*
  worst case scenarios
    failure to gather records ... *41*

E-mail ... *66, 67*
Electronic Communications Privacy Act ... *66*
Elements of investigations *18*

Employee assistance program ... *135*
Equal treatment ... *22, 127*
  worst case scenarios
    immediate dismissal ... *22*
    inconsistent treatment ... *37*

Fact finding ... *39*
Fair Credit Reporting Act ... *24, 54, 118, 134*
  best practices
    consumer credit report procedures ... *24*
Follow up ... *137*

Good faith ... *22, 122*
Guidelines for investigations ... *19*

Handbooks ... *62*
Harassment
  best practices
    adequate response ... *126*
  checklists
    harassment determination ... *111*
  interview ... *82*
  policy ... *125*
  worst case scenario
    continuing harassment ... *138*
Hearsay ... *92*

Interim actions ... *29*
Interviews
  accused's interview ... *85*
  best practices
    model interview ... *88*
  checklists
    dos and don'ts ... *74*
  complaining employee's interview ... *82*
  confirmation memo ... *84, 102*
  congruent communication ... *75*
  dos and don'ts ... *74*
  generally ... *62*
  harassment claim ... *82*
  hearsay ... *92*
  how to structure questions ... *90*

Index

leading questions ... *91*
location of ... *80*
order of interviews ... *75*
questions to avoid ... *91*
refusals
   accused ... *79*
   Garrity rule ... *80*
   victim ... *80*
representation during interview
   attorney ... *78*
   complainant's request ... *79*
   coworker's role ... *77*
   employee ... *76*
   friends or family ... *79*
telephone ... *81*
tips ... *82*
who to interview ... *44*
witness interviews ... *87*
worst case scenarios
   observable interview ... *81*
   reluctant witness ... *53*
Investigative tools—*see also Interviews, Polygraph tests, Searches*
   best practices
      plan preparation ... *36*
   checklists
      plan preparation ... *35*
   drug testing ... *69*
   interviews ... *62*
   polygraph testing ... *67*
   searches ... *62*
Investigators
   best practices
      number of investigators ... *57*
   checklists
      characteristics, good ... *52*
      outside investigators, advantages of ... *54*
      who not to select ... *49*
   communication skills ... *50*
   identity ... *20*
   impartiality ... *48*

legal advisors ... *55*
legal requirements ... *49*
number of ... *57*
outside investigators ... *52*
staff members ... *51*

Medical records—*see under Documentation*
Miranda rights ... *21, 77*

Need to know basis ... *20, 42, 106, 118*
Notes
   employee "sign off" ... *103*
   note-taking ... *92, 101*
   tape recorded ... *93, 102*

Polygraph records—*see under Documentation*
Polygraph tests
   definition ... *67*
   federal law coverage ... *68*
   ongoing investigation exemption ... *67, 68*
   procedural requirements ... *69*
   prohibition ... *67*
   record retention ... *106*
Privacy
   best practices
      expectation management ... *61*
   Electronic Communications Privacy Act ... *66*
   managing expectations ... *60*
   policy ... *61*
Prompt action ... *11, 19, 128*

Reasons for investigations ... *7*
Recommendations ... *112, 116, 123*
Records—*see Documentation*
Report
   appendices ... *117*
   components ... *116*
   conclusions ... *117*
   destruction of drafts ... *117*
   distribution ... *117*
   factual findings ... *116*

legal advisor's approval ... *117*
preliminary ... *115*
Representation during interview—*see
under Interviews*
Retaliation
  checklist
    responses to retaliation ... *132*
  defined ... *131*
  liability ... *131*
  prevention ... *6*

Searches
  business need ... *63*
  checklists
    e-mail ... *67*
    implementation ... *64*
    persons ... *66*
    policy communication ... *63*
    property
      electronics ... *66*
      employee's ... *65*
      employer's ... *66*
    reasonableness ... *63*
    witnesses ... *64*
  worst case scenarios
    surreptitious search ... *27*
Standard of proof ... *112*

Substance abuse
  indicators ... *71*
  worst case scenarios
    drinking on the job ... *70*

Tape recorders ... *69, 93, 102*
Transfers ... *115, 127*
Type of investigation
  accident ... *6*
  formal or informal ... *11*

Voice mail
  search ... *66*

Weingarten rights—*see also representation
during interview under Interviews*
  generally ... *76, 77*
Written statements ... *84, 85, 102, 117*
Worst case scenarios
  continuing harassment ... *138*
  delayed response ... *8*
  drinking on the job ... *70*
  failure to gather records ... *41*
  immediate dismissal ... *22*
  inconsistent treatment ... *37*
  observable interview ... *81*
  reluctant witness ... *53*
  surreptitious search ... *27*